The Way of a Pilgrim

and

The Pilgrim Continues His Way

The Way of a Pilgrim

and

The Pilgrim Continues His Way

New Sarov Press
1997

Printed with the blessing
of
His Grace Bishop HILARION
Russian Orthodox Church
Outside of Russia

Translation of *The Way of a Pilgrim* by George P. Fedotov
Originally published by Sheed and Ward Copyright 1950

Translation of *The Pilgrim Continues His Way* by R. M. French.
Translation Copyright 1965

New Sarov Press, Blanco, Texas 78606

First Impression: 1994
Second Impression: 1997

06 05 04   10 9 8 7 6 5 4 3

New Sarov Press
Christ of the Hills Monastery
Blanco, Texas 78606-1049
USA

ISBN 1-880364-12-3

Contents

Acknowledgment

With deepest gratitude to Catherine Penn, Malcolm McElvaney, and Sandra Jones Edwards without whose help this book could not have been published.

Foreword

Sometimes in life you have an experience or read a book that resonates in the depths of your soul. It is almost like walking into a room and feeling as though you have been there before. You know where everything is and it is as though you have seen it all before. Years later the memory is almost as vivid as the incident. It was like this the first time someone taught me the Jesus Prayer. I was a young boy, twelve or thirteen years of age, and it was a bright early autumn day. It is with me even now.

Today I am a Monk in the twilight years of my life. My whole life was changed because of this Prayer. I spent my life searching with all my heart to deepen this experience. This search began the day after I first learned the Prayer. I spoke to my friend who had taught me the Jesus Prayer and asked to know more about it, and he gave me the little book The Way of a Pilgrim and the Pilgrim Continues His Way. Since that time, I have read this book perhaps fifty times in my life. Each time it is new. Each time there are discoveries that are unfolding almost as though for the very first time. This is the remarkable mystery that this little book, The Way of A Pilgrim, opens up in the heart of someone seeking to pray without ceasing.

For years I prayed this Prayer quietly on my own. And some years later when I was a young man, I entered a Benedictine Monastery. There, when I was a Novice, there was someone who knew a little bit about the Jesus Prayer. I was deeply touched by this knowledge of the Prayer and learned about the Orthodox prayer rope or chotki. Since no one was able to teach me how to tie the knots, I began to make the prayer ropes by stringing beads and tying knots between each decade. I sought to know more about the Jesus Prayer and to find a copy of the *Philokalia*, but at that point there were no translations of any part of it yet available in English.

Many years later, the treasure of the *Philokalia* became available, first in selected sections that dealt specifically with the Jesus Prayer, and then as the later volumes of Bishop Kallistos Ware's work began to appear, the entire *Philokalia* began to unfold. It only made me feel further lost, however. I was looking for someone, an Elder (*Starets* or *Geronta*), who could help me with this. Everything I read described the importance of such a person. I began to teach the Jesus Prayer myself to Monks who were, at this point in my life, under my care. And I began to realize how woefully short I fell from what they needed. And so the search for a Spiritual Father intensified. We began to pray to God to lead us to some kind of a Spiritual Father who could help us. No where in the West could we find such a person. We began to pray that God would find us an Orthodox Starets or Geronta. This seemed even more remote. When we asked Orthodox Christians about such a possibility they smiled and said there were no more Startsi or that there were very few Elders left on earth, and that perhaps we should go to Mount Athos.

We intensified our prayer to God to find such a Spiritual Father for us. Finally, we began to pray to God to take away everything that stood in the way and tried to simplify our lives to live more and more like those first Monks who went out into the desert. We chose to literally live the Rule of St. Benedict just as it was written, and we began to fast and to pray again more fervently.

Foreword

Finally, by a set of circumstances that would take an entire book to tell by themselves, God answered this prayer. This led us directly into the question of the Orthodox Church. My Spiritual Father was very gentle and did not at all insist that we become Orthodox at first, but simply tried to answer our questions about the Prayer and to give out some very simple and basic advise about the Jesus Prayer. He did tell us, however, that if we continued to practice it, we would become Orthodox, because nothing else would satisfy us. He said he did not have to speak to us about this because our hearts would grow to yearn for Holy Orthodoxy, and that we would ask him to instruct us and to make us Orthodox when we were ready. He was right. Before long, we were begging to understand more and our hearts ached to be Orthodox. We wanted to be part of the Orthodox Church more than anything in the world. He granted our request and made us Orthodox, and we began to experience the tremendous depths of the Eastern Orthodox mystical tradition.

Untold books could be written about all of this, but I am really not worthy to speak of it. And although these untold books could go on for thousands of pages, there really are no human words that can describe where this Prayer leads. All I can tell you is that the deepest desires of the human heart are fulfilled in this Prayer. And that this Prayer will lead you to an experience of God so profound and so totally all-embracing that there are not words to describe it.

As I speak these words to you who are beginning for the first time to open the treasure that this little book will be, I find myself obligated to tell you that if you begin to practice this Prayer it will make you Orthodox. I must caution you to try to find someone to help you

Foreword

with this Prayer, particularly if you begin to advance in its practice. I do not recommend that you try to plumb the depths of the *Philokalia* without a sure guide and without the advise of a Spiritual Father into whose hands I urge you to abandon yourself with the pure trust of a child in the hands of its parent. Be careful whom you choose. There are many frauds and charlatans about. Look for someone who is humble. Humility is an icon of truth that does not coexist with those whose motives are not pure. Look for someone who is simple, and in some ways innocent. A man cannot enter into the Kingdom of Heaven unless he becomes like a little child. If you are blessed enough to find someone to help you--you cannot imagine how far this Prayer will lead you.

Struggle to repent for your sins. A person must be able to look at himself with total honesty. We will all stand naked before God on Judgement Day. If you would encounter God even now in your life, you must begin with this honesty and you must gradually tame the old man. For this it is necessary to pray and to fast. The fasts of the Orthodox Church are rigorous, but I urge you to take on not only the literal observance of the fast, but the spirit of the fast so that it may transform your heart. This humility and repentance, coupled with devoted obedience to your Spiritual Father, the frequent reception of the Holy Mysteries (Sacraments), and the practice of the Jesus Prayer will lead you to the very heart of God. It is a journey beyond words.

Fr. Benedict

Introduction
"The Pilgrim" On Mental Prayer
by George P. Fedotov

The Candid Narrations of a Pilgrim to His Spiritual Father was first printed in Kazan in 1884. It soon became a rare book, considered to be almost esoteric and held in high esteem by all searchers into the ways of Orthodox mysticism. Only recently, through reprinting in Western Europe and translation into English, has this precious little book become accessible to the wide circle interested in Russian religious life.

Nothing is known of the author. Written in the first person singular, the book presents itself as the spiritual autobiography of a Russian peasant who lived at about the middle of the nineteenth century, related in intimate conversations. The social conditions depicted in the story represent Russia during the last decades of serfdom, under the severe autocratic government of Nicholas I. The mention made of the Crimean War (1853-54) permits an exact chronological placement.

There are, however, many factors which do not allow us to accept literally the anonymous author's description of himself. Although the style of the book has somewhat the flavor of the popular Russian idiom, it is essentially in the elaborate literary manner characteristic of the Russian spiritual writing of the middle of the nineteenth century. There are even many traces of the epoch of Alexandrian mysticism (Alexander I, 1801-1825) which deeply influenced the religious mentality and style of the Russian Church. Quite apart from the style, we come across many profound theological and philosophical digressions and comments which would be inconceivable in the mouth of a Russian peasant, even one well read in the *Philokalia*. The traces of a romanticism of Western origin are undeniable.

On the other hand, the many incidents related in detail, and even the confused order of the narrative, prevent us from dismissing the autobiographical form of the narration wholly as a literary convention. Probably a real experience of the pilgrim is the basis of the composition. Some educated person may have worked over the original oral confessions, either his actual "spiritual father," a Priest or Monk in Irkutsk (Siberia), or some Monk on Mount Athos, whence the manuscript is supposed to have been brought to Kazan by the Abbot Paísius.

These critical remarks are intended to warn the reader not to accept the mystical life of the Pilgrim as reflecting Russian popular religion. On the contrary, it is the product of a fine spiritual culture, a rare flower in the Russian garden. Its main value consists in a convincingly detailed description of mental prayer as it was or could be practiced, not in a monastic cell, but by a layman, even under the peculiar conditions of a wandering life.

From another point of view, the book is a work of propaganda, designed to popularize in lay circles the mystical prayer of the Hesychasts as embodied in an ascetic-mystical anthology entitled the *Philokalia*. The first Greek edition of this anthology, the work of an anonymous compiler (probably Saint Nicodemus of Mount Athos), was printed in Venice in 1782. The Slavonic translation by Saint Paísius Velichkovsky was printed in 1793. Most of the Greek Fathers of this collection were already known in Russia to Saint Nilus Sorsky in the fifteenth century. But from the sixteenth century onward, the mystical movement in Russia was suppressed until the time of the revival effected by Paísius. This Russian Monk was an ,émigré, living in the Balkan Monasteries of Mount Athos and Romania, where he imbibed the mystical tradition at its sources. The whole monastic revival which took form at the end of the eighteenth and the beginning of the nineteenth century in Russia is attributable to Paísius and his disciples. The Optina cloister in Russia (in the province of Kaluga), with its unbroken line of Startzy, held itself to be the heir and depository in a special sense of Paísius' tradition.

That this tradition was not held within the confines of Monasteries is demonstrated by the Pilgrim's book. It is his aim to convince us that mental prayer is possible in every condition of life. True, he admits that complete solitude is for him the most favorable condition for the practice of continual prayer: he often feels uneasy in human society when suddenly the Prayer of Jesus begins to "act of itself" in his heart. Yet the conditions under which a wanderer lives are as suitable for mystical prayer as is the cell of a Monk.

The wandering life (this is a more correct English equivalent of the Russian phrase than "pilgrimage") is characteristic of Russian spirituality. Very often, as in the case of the present author, the wandering has no visit to a place of devotion as its object but is a way of life in which the early Christian ideal of spiritual freedom and detachment from the world is grafted on the Russian feeling for the religious significance of nature as Mother Earth, and the truly Russian rejection of civilization out of religious motives. Yet, reading the tales of the Pilgrim, we realize that the mystical life of the author is moving against a background of the

15

Introduction

external manifestations of Christian charity. Some of his tales have little or nothing to do with the Prayer of Jesus, but portray ideal types of the evangelical life, found in all strata of society--among the gentry, the army, the clergy, the simple peasantry. These portraits of secular, uncanonized, and even unknown, lay saints are, as it were, a counterpoint to the scenes of cruelty, violence, and despotism which we are not spared. What is lacking is rather the average level of Russian life. The author has not the intention of depicting life around him as it is, but that of selecting instructive examples of Christian virtue.

The Way of a Pilgrim

The Way of a Pilgrim

Chapter I

By the grace of God I am a Christian, by my deeds a great sinner, and by calling a homeless rover of the lowest status in life. My possessions comprise but some rusk in a knapsack on my back, and the Holy Bible on my bosom. That is all.

On the twenty-fourth Sunday after Pentecost, I went to church to attend Divine Liturgy. The first Epistle of St. Paul to the Thessalonians was read. In it we are exhorted, among other things, to pray unceasingly, and these words engraved themselves upon my mind. I began to ponder whether it is possible to pray without ceasing, since every man must occupy himself with other things needed for his support. I found this text in my Bible and read with my own eyes what I had heard, namely that we must pray unceasingly in all places, pray always in spirit, lifting up our hands in devotion. I pondered and pondered and did not know what to think of it.

"What am I to do?" I mused. "Where will I be able to find someone who can explain it to me? I shall go to the churches known for their famous preachers; perhaps there I shall hear something that will enlighten me." And I went. I heard a great many very good sermons on prayer in general, how one ought to pray, what prayer is and what fruits it bears, but no one said how to succeed in it. There were sermons on spiritual prayer, on unceasing prayer, but no one pointed out how it was to be accomplished.

The Way of A Pilgrim

Thus my attendance at the sermons failed to give me what I sought. Therefore, after having heard many of them, I gave them up without acquiring the desired knowledge of unceasing prayer. I decided to look, with the help of God, for an experienced and learned man who would talk to me and explain the meaning of unceasing prayer since the understanding of it seemed most important to me.

For a long time I went from one place to another, reading my Bible constantly, and inquiring everywhere whether there was not a spiritual teacher or a pious and experienced guide. Finally, I was informed that in a certain village there lived a gentleman who had, for many years, sought the salvation of his soul. He had a chapel in his house, never left the premises and spent his days praying and reading religious books. Upon hearing this I well-nigh ran to that particular village. I got there and went to the owner of the estate.

"What is it that you want?" he asked.

"I was told that you are a pious and intelligent man," I said. "For the love of God enlighten me in the meaning of the Apostle's utterance 'pray unceasingly.' Is it possible for anyone to pray without ceasing? I wish I could know, but I do not seem to understand it at all."

The gentleman remained silent for a while, looking at me fixedly. Finally he said: "Unceasing inner prayer is a continuous longing of the human spirit for God. But in order to succeed in this sweet practice we must pray more and ask God to teach us unceasing prayer. Pray more and with fervor. It is prayer itself that will teach you how it can be done without ceasing; however, it will require some time."

Having said this he ordered that food be brought to me, gave me money for my journey and dismissed me. And in the end he had explained nothing at all.

Once more I set out. I pondered and pondered, read and read, and my thoughts dwelt constantly upon what this man had told me, though I could not understand what he meant. Yet, so ardently did I wish to fathom this question, that I could not sleep at night.

I traveled two hundred *versts*[1] on foot and reached a large city which was the capital of the province. There I saw a Monastery, and at the inn where I stayed I learned that the abbot was a kindly man, at once pious and hospitable. When I went to see him he received me in a friendly fashion, asked me to sit down and offered refreshments.

"Holy father," I said, "I do not want any food, but I beg you, enlighten me in spiritual matters. Tell me how I can save my soul."

"How can you save your soul? Well, live according to the commandments, pray and you will be saved."

"But it is said that we should pray unceasingly. I do not know how this can be done for I cannot even get the meaning of it. Father, I beseech you, explain to me what unceasing prayer means."

"I do not know, dear brother, how to explain it to you! But wait a moment... I have a little book which

---

[1] A *verst* is almost two thirds of a mile.

will enlighten you." He handed me St. Demetrius' book called The Spiritual Education of the Inner Man and said: "Here, read this page."

I read the following statement: "The words of the Apostle 'pray unceasingly' should be interpreted as referring to the prayer of the mind, for the mind can always be soaring to God and pray without ceasing."

"But," I said, "won't you indicate to me the means by which the mind can always be directed to God without being disturbed in its unceasing prayer?"

"This, indeed, is very difficult, unless God Himself bestows upon one such a gift," answered the abbot, and he offered no further explanations.

I spent the night in his Monastery. The following morning I thanked him for his kind hospitality and went on my way, though I did not know myself where I was going. I was saddened by my incapacity to understand and read the Holy Bible for consolation.

In this wise I followed the main road for about five days when, one evening, I was overtaken by an elderly man who looked as though he belonged to the clergy. In reply to my question he answered that he was a Monk from a Monastery situated some ten *versts* off the main road and extended to me his invitation.

"In our guesthouse," he said, "we offer rest, shelter and food to pilgrims and other pious people." I did not care to go with him and replied that my peace of mind did not depend upon my lodging, but upon finding spiritual guidance. Neither was I concerned about my food, for I had a provision of rusk in my knapsack.

"What kind of spiritual guidance are you seeking? What is it that troubles you?" he asked. "Do come for a short stay, dear brother. We have experienced elders who will guide you and lead you to the true path in the light of the word of God and the teaching of the Holy Fathers."

I told him what was troubling me. The old man crossed himself and said: "Give thanks to God, my beloved brother, for he has awakened you to the irresistible longing for unceasing, inner prayer. Acknowledge in it the voice of our Lord and be calm in the assurance that all that has happened to you hitherto was the testing of the compliance of your own will with the call of God. You have been given the privilege of understanding that the heavenly light of unceasing inner prayer is not found in worldly wisdom or in mere striving for outward knowledge. On the contrary, it is attained in poverty of spirit, in active experience and in simplicity of heart. For this reason it is not astonishing that you have not been able to learn anything about the essential work of prayer or to attain the skill by which unceasing activity in it is acquired. What is prayer and how does one learn to pray? Though these questions are vital and essential, one gets only rarely a true enlightenment on that subject from contemporary preachers. It is because these questions are more complex than all the arguments they have at their disposal. These questions require not merely academic achievements, but mystical insight. And one of the most lamentable things is the vanity of elementary knowledge which drives people to measure the Divine by a human yardstick. Only too often wrong reasoning is applied to

The Way of A Pilgrim

prayer, for many believe that preparatory steps and great virtues lead us to prayer. In fact it is prayer that gives birth to all the virtues and sublime deeds. The fruits and consequences of prayer are wrongly taken for the means of attaining it. This attitude belittles the value of prayer, and it is contrary to the statements of the Holy Scripture. The Apostle Paul says: 'I desire therefore, first of all, that supplications be made.' Here the main thing that the Apostle stressed in his words about prayer is that prayer must come before anything else: 'I desire therefore, first of all'. There are many virtues that are required of a good Christian, but above all else he must pray; for nothing can ever be achieved without prayer. Otherwise he cannot find his way to God, he cannot grasp the truth, he cannot crucify the flesh with all its passions and desires, find the Light of Christ in his heart and be united to our Lord. Frequent prayer must precede all these things before they can be brought about. I say 'frequent because the perfection and the correctness of prayer is beyond our power. 'For we know not what we should pray for as we ought,' says the Apostle Paul. Therefore we ought to pray often, to pray at all times, for this alone lies within our power and leads us to purity of prayer, which is the mother of all spiritual good. As St. Isaac the Syrian says: 'Win the mother and she will bear you children,' so must you first of all attain the power of prayer, and then all other virtues will be easily practiced afterwards. All this is scarcely mentioned by those who have had no personal experience, but only a superficial knowledge of the most mysterious teaching of the Holy Fathers,"

While he talked to me, we reached the Monastery without noticing it. In order that I might not lose contact with this wise elder, and to get further information more quickly, I hastened to say: "Reverend Father, do me a favor: Explain to me what unceasing prayer is, and how I am to learn it. As I see, you are deeply versed in all these matters."

It was with kindness that he granted my request and taking me to his cell, he said: "Come in, I shall give you a book written by the Holy Fathers. With God's help you may get from it a clear and definite idea of what prayer is."

As we entered his cell he began to speak again: "The constant inner Prayer of Jesus is an unbroken, perpetual calling upon the Divine Name of Jesus with the lips, the mind and the heart, while picturing His lasting presence in one's imagination and imploring His grace wherever one is, in whatever one does, even while one sleeps. This Prayer consists of the following words: - 'Lord Jesus Christ, have mercy on me!' Those who use this prayer constantly are so greatly comforted that they are moved to say it at all times, for they can no longer live without it. And the prayer will keep on ringing in their hearts of its own accord. Now, do you understand what unceasing prayer is?"

"Yes, I do, Father. In the Name of God explain to me how to achieve the mastery of it," I said, feeling overwhelmed with joy.

"You will learn how to master it by reading this book, which is called the *Philokalia*[2]; it comprises the complete and minute knowledge of unceasing inner prayer, as stated by twenty-five Holy Fathers. It is full

---

[2] *Philokalia* (in Russian: *Dobrotolyubie*). "The Love of Spiritual Beauty." The title of the great collection of mystical and ascetic writings by Fathers of the Eastern Orthodox Church, over a period of eleven centuries.

of great wisdom and is so useful that it is regarded as the first and best guide by all those who seek the contemplative, spiritual life. The Venerable Nicephorus said once: 'It leads one to salvation without labor and sweat.'"

"Is it then loftier and holier than the Bible?" I asked.

"No, it is not, but it sheds light upon the secrets locked up in the Bible which cannot be easily understood by our shallow intelligence. Let me give you an analogy: the largest, the brightest and at the same time the most wonderful of all luminaries is the sun; yet you must protect your eyes in order to examine it, or simply to look at it. For this purpose you use artificial glass, millions and millions of times smaller and darker than the sun. But through this tiny piece of glass you can contemplate the sublime king of all stars with its flamboyant rays. Thus the Holy Scripture is like the resplendent sun, while this book—the *Philokalia*—may be compared to the piece of glass which permits us to contemplate its lofty magnificence. Now, listen; I shall read you the instructions on unceasing prayer as they are given here."

He opened the book, and after having found the instruction by St. Simeon the New Theologian, he began to read: "Take a seat in solitude and silence. Bend your head, close your eyes, and breathing softly, in your imagination, look into your own heart. Let your mind, or rather, your thoughts, flow from your head down to your heart and say, while breathing: 'Lord Jesus Christ, have mercy on me.' Whisper these words gently, or say them in your mind. Discard all other thoughts. Be serene, persevering and repeat them over and over again."

The elder did not limit himself to mere explanations, but made them clear by examples. We read passages of St. Gregory of Sinai, St. Callistus and St. Ignatius and he interpreted them to me in his own words. I listened to him attentively, overwhelmed with gladness, and did my best to store every detail in my memory. Thus we stayed up the whole night together and went to Matins without having slept at all.

When the elder dismissed me with his blessings, he told me that while I was learning the ways of prayer I must return and relate to him my experiences in a full and sincere Confession; for this work cannot be crowned with success except with the attentive guidance of a teacher.

In the church I felt a burning zeal to practice unceasing prayer diligently and asked God to help me. Then I began to ask myself how I could visit the elder for guidance and Confession, since it was not permitted to remain in the Monastery guesthouse for more than three days, and there were no other houses nearby.

However, I soon discovered a village situated about four *versts* from the Monastery. When I went there in search of living quarters, God led me to the right place. A peasant engaged me for the whole summer to take care of his kitchen garden; he placed at my disposal a hut where I could live by myself. Praise be to God! I came upon a quiet place! I took up my dwelling and began to learn inner prayer in the manner I had been told and went to see my elder from time to time.

The Way of A Pilgrim

Alone in my garden, I practiced unceasing prayer for a week as the elder had directed me. In the beginning things went very well. But soon I began to feel tired, lazy and bored. Overcome by drowsiness, I was often distracted by all kinds of thoughts that came upon me like a cloud. I went to see my elder in great anxiety and told him of my plight.

He received me cordially and said: "The kingdom of darkness assails you, my dear brother. To it nothing is worse than a Prayer of the Heart. And the kingdom of darkness uses every means at its disposal to hold you back and to prevent you from learning prayer. Nevertheless the fiend can do no more than God will permit, no more than is needed for our own good. It seems that your humility needs more testing; it is too soon for you to approach with intemperate zeal the sublime entrance of the heart, lest you fall into spiritual covetousness. Let me read you an instruction from the *Philokalia* about this case."

The elder found the teaching of Nicephorus the Monk, and began to read: "If after some efforts you do not succeed in reaching the region of the heart in the manner you have been told, do what I am about to tell you, and with the help of God you will find what you are seeking. The faculty of speech is located in the larynx, as you know. Drive back all other thoughts - you can do it if you wish - and use that faculty in saying constantly the following words: 'Lord Jesus Christ, have mercy on me.' Make yourself do so at all times. If you persist in it for a while, your heart by this means will be open to prayer without doubt. This is known from experience."

The Way of A Pilgrim

"Here you have the teaching of Holy Fathers dealing with these cases," said the elder. "Therefore you must accept it with confidence and repeat the oral Jesus Prayer as often as possible. Take this chotki[3]. Use it in saying three thousand prayers every day in the beginning. Whether you sit or stand, walk or lie down, constantly repeat: 'Lord Jesus Christ, have mercy on me.' Do it quietly, without hurrying, but say it exactly three thousand times a day, neither increasing nor diminishing the number of prayers of your own accord. By this means God will help you to attain also the unceasing action of the heart."

With joy I accepted this instruction and returned to my lodging, where I began to carry out faithfully and exactly what the elder ordered me to do. It was somewhat hard for two days. Later it became so easy and pleasant that I felt something like a longing for the prayer; I said it willingly and cheerfully, and not under compulsion as before.

I told my elder of this and he decreed that I recite six thousand prayers a day: "Be calm," he admonished me, "and try to say as faithfully as possible the fixed number of prayers. The Lord in His mercy will give you His grace."

In my solitary hut I said for a whole week the Jesus Prayer six thousand times a day, forgetting all cares and discarding all other thoughts, however much they assailed me. I had in mind but the one aim of fulfilling the bidding of the elder faithfully. And, behold! I got so used to my prayer that when I stopped for a short time I felt as if I was missing something, as if I had undergone a loss. And the minute I started it all over again I had

---

[3] *Chotki.* A prayer rope with knots or beads for counting prayers.

the joyous sensation of freedom. When I met people, I did not care to enter into conversation at all, for all I desired was to be left alone and to say my prayer, so accustomed had I grown to it during that week.

The elder, who had not seen me for about ten days, called on me himself. I told him how I was getting along. He listened attentively and then said: "Now that you have become accustomed to prayer, persist in this habit and strengthen it. Waste no time, and with the help of God say precisely twelve thousand prayers a day from now on. Keep to yourself, get up early, go to bed later than usual, and come to me for advice twice a month.

I did as the elder ordered me to do. On the first day I had barely finished my twelve thousand prayers by the late evening. But the following day they flowed with greater ease and joy. At first the unceasing saying of the prayer wearied me to a certain extent; my tongue was somewhat numbed and my jaws stiff. My palate, too, hurt a little, but this was not unpleasant at all. I felt a slight pain in the thumb of my left hand, which I used for counting my beads. A minor inflammation developed in my left arm from the wrist up to the elbow. The sensation it caused was most pleasant; it stimulated and urged me to the frequent saying of the prayer. Thus for about five days I said faithfully my twelve thousand prayers, and as the habit became fixed I did it willingly and with joy.

Early one morning I was, so to speak, aroused by the prayer. When I began to recite my morning prayers, my tongue refused to utter the familiar words with ease. My only desire was to go on with the Jesus Prayer, and no sooner had I started it than I felt joyfully relieved. My lips and my tongue recited the words without any effort on my part. I spent the whole day experiencing great happiness and a complete detachment from earthly things, as though I were living on another planet. Easily did I finish my twelve thousand prayers by the early evening. I wished I might keep on, but I dared not to increase the number fixed by my elder. The following day I continued in the same way, calling on the Name of Jesus Christ, and did it with readiness and facility. Then I went to see the elder and, opening my heart, I told him everything in detail.

He listened to me attentively and then began to speak: "Thank God for having discovered in yourself the desire and facility for prayer. This is a natural result that crowns continuous efforts and action. It is like this: a machine operates for a while if its principal wheel is given a push; however, if it is to operate still longer, that wheel must be oiled and given another push. And so is the sensual nature of man, which God in His loving mercy has endowed with great capacities. You have yourself experienced what a feeling can be born in a sinful soul not yet in the state of grace, not yet purified from all sensuality. But how comforting, wonderful and sublime it is when God in His benevolence cleanses the soul of man from passion and bestows upon him the gift of self-acting, spiritual prayer! This state is impossible to describe, for the revelation of the mystery of prayer foretells here on earth the bliss of heaven. That kind of happiness is granted to loving hearts which seek after God in simplicity. Now I authorize you to recite the Prayer as often as you wish, the more the better. Give it all your waking hours, and from now on call on the Name of Jesus without counting. Submit yourself to the will of God in humility, looking to Him for assistance. I

firmly believe that He will not abandon you but direct
your steps."

Following these instructions I spent the whole
summer in unceasing oral prayer to Jesus, enjoying
peace of mind and soul. I often dreamt in my sleep that I
was reciting the Prayer. If during the day I happened to
meet people, I felt that I liked them as though they were
my closest relatives, but I wasted none of my time on
them. My thoughts calmed down by themselves. I was
concerned with nothing but my Prayer, to which my
mind was beginning to listen; and from time to time the
sensation of delightful warmth was sweeping over my
heart. Whenever I went to church the long monastic
services seemed short to me and failed to tire me out as
had happened before. And my lonely hut had for me all
the splendor of a palace. I did not know how to thank
God for having guided me, a miserable sinner, to that
saving elder who became my master.

However, I was not long to profit by the instructions
of my beloved teacher, who was blessed with divine
wisdom. At the end of the summer he passed away. I
bade him my last farewell in tears and in profound
gratitude for the fatherly guidance he had given to a
poor wretch like myself. For a blessing I begged
permission to keep the chotki which he had been using
in his prayers.

Thus I remained alone. Summer passed and the work
in the kitchen garden came to an end. My peasant
dismissed me, giving me two rubles for my work as a
watchman and filling up my knapsack with rusk for my
journey. Once more I set off on my wanderings to
various places. But now I was no longer alone and in
want as before. Calling upon the Name of Jesus brought

cheer to me on my way. People I met were kind to me as if they liked me.

Thus I began to wonder what to do with the money I had earned for my work in the kitchen garden. What was it good for? "Look here," I said to myself. My elder was gone. I had no one to guide me. Why not buy the *Philokalia* with the purpose of learning from it more about inner prayer.

I made the sign of the cross and went on my way reciting my Prayer. When I came to a large province town I began to look for the *Philokalia* in all the stores. Finally I found the book, but they asked me three rubles for it, whereas I had only two in my possession. I haggled and haggled over the price, but the shopkeeper would not give in. In the end he suggested: "Go to that church nearby and speak to the warden. He has a very old copy of this book and may be willing to sell it to you for two rubles." I made my way there and lo! for my two rubles I bought the *Philokalia*. It was an old copy, much damaged by use. Overjoyed with my purchase, I repaired it as well as I could, made a cloth cover for it, and put it into my knapsack with the Bible.

And now, I am wandering about repeating unceasingly the Prayer of Jesus. To me it has greater value than anything else on earth. Occasionally I walk seventy *versts* or so and do not feel it at all. I am conscious of only one thing, my Prayer. When bitter cold pierces me, I say it more eagerly and warm up in no time. When I am hungry I begin to call on the Name of Jesus more often and forget about food. When I am ill and rheumatic pains set in my back and legs, I concentrate on the Prayer and no longer notice the discomfort. When people do me wrong, my wrath and indignation are quickly forgotten as soon as I remember the sweetness of the Prayer of Jesus. In a way I have become a half-witted person; I have no anxiety and no interest in the vanities of the world, for which I care no longer. I am longing by habit for only one thing, to be left alone and to pray unceasingly. When I am doing this I am filled with joy. God knows what is going on within me. It is sensuous, no doubt! As my departed elder explained to me, this is natural and artificial at the same time, as a consequence of my daily practice. But I realize my lack of merit and of intelligence and dare not proceed further in learning and mastering the spiritual prayer within my heart. God will enlighten me at the same time. Meanwhile, I hope that my late elder prays for me. Though I have not yet reached the state in which ceaseless spiritual prayer is self-acting in the heart, I do understand, thank God, the meaning of the Apostle's words in the Epistle: "Pray unceasingly."

Chapter II

I roamed about through many different places for a long time with the Prayer of Jesus as my sole companion. It gladdened and comforted me in all my wanderings, my meetings with other people and in all the incidents of the journey. Soon, however, it occurred to me that it would be better to take a fixed abode so as to be alone more often and study the *Philokalia* more easily. Though I read this book whenever I could in all the refuges I was able to find for the night's or day's rest, I felt that I ought to dedicate more time to it. With faith and concentration I wished to gather from its instruction more information about the truth that would save my soul by means of inner prayer.

But despite my sincere desire I could not find any work whatever, for my left arm was crippled from early childhood. Because of this I was not able to make a permanent home for myself. Thus I made up my mind to go to Siberia and to visit the tomb of St. Innocent in Irkutsk. I thought that I would travel in the great silence of Siberian forests and steppes in a manner that was more suitable for praying and reading. I set off and on my way recited the Prayer without ceasing.

At the end of a short period I began to feel that the Prayer had, so to speak, passed to my heart. In other words I felt that my heart in its natural beating began, as it were, to utter the words of the Prayer. For instance, one "Lord"; two "Jesus"; three Christ, and so forth. No longer did I say the Prayer with my lips, but listened attentively to the words formed in my heart, remembering what my departed elder told me about this state of bliss. Then I began to feel a slight pain in my heart, and my whole being was glowing with so great a

The Way of A Pilgrim

love for Jesus Christ that it seemed to me if only I could meet Him, I would fall to His feet, embracing them and kissing them in tenderness, tears and gratitude for His love and mercy which gives such comfort in calling on His Name to me, His unworthy creature. A pleasant warmth was filling my heart and spreading through my whole bosom. This urged me to a more eager reading of the *Philokalia*, so as to test my emotions and to study further the effects of inner prayer. Without this test I might have fallen a victim of delusion, or might have taken natural results for the manifestation of grace, and prided myself at the quick mastering of the Prayer. My late elder had warned me of this danger. I decided therefore to walk more at night and to devote my days mainly to reading the *Philokalia*, sitting under the forest trees. Ah! A wisdom so great that I had never thought it possible was revealed to me in this reading. As I went on, I felt a happiness which, until then, had been beyond my imagination. Although many passages were still incomprehensible to my dull mind, the Prayer of the Heart brought the understanding I wanted. Besides, on rare occasions, I dreamt of my late elder, who explained many things to me, and, above all, led my dormant soul to the path of humility.

Thus, blissfully happy, I spent more than two months of the summer. As a general rule I made my way through the forest, choosing byways. Whenever I entered a village I asked only for rusk and a little salt. With my bark jar filled with water I made another hundred *versts*.

Summer was drawing to a close as I was assailed with trials and temptations. Were they the consequence of sins weighing on my wretched soul? Or was something lacking in my spiritual life which required other experiences? I do not know. This is what happened: One day, at twilight, when I reached the main road, two men looking like soldiers caught up with me and demanded money. When I told them that I had not a penny on me, they refused to believe me and shouted rudely: "You are lying. Pilgrims always collect plenty of money."

"What is the use of talking to him," said one of them, and he hit me on the head with his club with such force that I fell senseless to the ground. How long I remained unconscious I do not know, but when I came to myself I was lying by the forest road, robbed. My knapsack was gone from my back; only the cords which had fastened it and which they had cut, remained. Thank God! they had not taken my passport, for I kept it in my old cap, ready to show it at a moment's notice. I rose, shedding bitter tears, not so much on account of the pain in my head, as for the loss of the Bible and the *Philokalia*, which were in the stolen bag.

I did not cease to mourn and to wail day and night. Where was my Bible, which I had carried with me all this time and read since my early youth? Where was my *Philokalia*, which gave me so much enlightenment and consolation? Alas, I had lost my first and last treasures in life without having enjoyed them fully. It would have been better for me to have been killed on the spot, than to exist without spiritual food. There was no way of replacing these books now.

Heavily I dragged myself for two days, overcome by my calamity. Exhausted at the end of the third day, I fell to the ground and went to sleep in the shelter of a bush. And then I had a dream. I saw myself in the Monastery cell of my elder, lamenting over my loss. In his endeavor to console me the old man was saying: "You must learn therefrom detachment from worldly things for your greater progress towards heaven. All this has been allowed to come to pass so as to prevent you from slipping into mere enjoyment of spiritual sweetness. God wills that a Christian relinquish his desires, his attachments and his own will, so as to give himself entirely to the Divine Providence. God directs all events for the good of mankind, for 'He wills that all men should be saved.' Be of good cheer and trust that along with the temptation God provides also a way of escape. In a short time you will rejoice more than you grieve now."

As these words were spoken, I woke up, my strength returned and my soul was at peace, as though filled with the brightness of dawn. "God's will be done," I said, and, crossing myself, got up and went on my way. Once more the Prayer was self-acting in my heart as it had been before, and I walked serenely for three days.

All of a sudden I met a group of convicts escorted by soldiers. When I came closer I saw the two men who had robbed me. As they were in the outside row, I fell to their feet and asked them urgently to tell me where my books were. In the beginning they paid no attention to my plea; finally one of them said: "If you'll give us something, we'll tell you where your books are. Give us a ruble."

I swore that I would gladly give them a ruble, even if I had to beg it for the love of God, and offered to leave with them my passport in pawn. At this, they told me that my books might be found in one of the carriages that followed the convicts with other stolen things which had been found on them.

"Well, but how can I get them?"

"Speak to the officer in charge."

I rushed to the officer and told him what had happened.

"Do you mean to say that you can read the Bible?" he asked.

"Indeed, I can," I replied. "Not only can I read everything, but I can also write. You will see my name written on the Bible, which proves that it belongs to me. And here is my passport bearing the same name and surname."

The officer told me that the two villains were deserters and lived in a forest hut. They had plundered many people until a quick-witted driver, whose troika they were about to steal, had caught them the day before. "Very well," he added, "I will return your books if they are there, but won't you walk with us as far as our stopping place for the night? It will save me from halting men and carriages on your account." I willingly agreed to this, and while I walked at the side of his horse, we fell into conversation.

The officer impressed me as being a kind and upright man, no longer young. He wished to know who I was, where I came from and where I was planning to go. To all his questions I gave a frank reply, and so we came to the house which marked the journey's end for that day. The officer got my books, and returning them to me,

The Way of A Pilgrim

said: "Now that it is night, stay here; you may sleep in my entrance-hall." I stayed.

I was so happy to have my books again that I did not know how to thank God. I pressed them to my chest for such a long time that my hands got quite stiff. I wept from exultation, my heart beating with gladness. The officer looked at me fixedly and said: "I see that you are very fond of your Bible." My happiness was so great that I was not able to speak. He continued: "I, too, read the Gospel every day, brother." He took from his breast pocket a small book of the Gospels bound in silver. It was printed in Kiev. "Take a seat," he said. "Let me tell you what happened to me."

"Hey, there! bring us some supper," he ordered.

We sat down to the table and the officer told me his story.

I have been in the army since my early youth - not in a garrison, but in the field service. My superiors liked me, for I knew my business and fulfilled my duties as a second lieutenant conscientiously. But I was young and had many friends. Unfortunately, I took to the bottle so that my passion became a disease. As long as I remained sober, I was a reliable officer, but when I yielded to temptation I was good for nothing, sometimes for a period of six weeks. They stood me for a long time, but in the end, when, in a state of intoxication, I insulted my commanding officer, I was degraded and transferred to a garrison as a private soldier for three years. And I was warned that a still more severe punishment was in store for me if I did not reform and give up drinking. I was so miserable that all my efforts to control or to cure myself proved vain. When I was

felt nothing but disgust for alcohol and for twenty years have never tasted a drop of it.

I was so greatly changed that everyone noticed it with surprise. Three years later my commission was restored to me. In due time I got a promotion and finally rose to the rank of a captain. I am married. My wife is a good woman. We are well provided for and live comfortably, thank God! We help the poor as far as our means permit and shelter the pilgrims. My son is also an officer now - a good boy. Note this, after I was cured of alcoholism, I vowed to read the Gospels every day as long as I lived - one Gospel in every twenty-four hours, allowing nothing to stop me from doing it. When I am very busy and too tired to do it myself, I relax and ask my wife or my son to read one Gospel to me, so that I may avoid breaking my vow.

I ordered a binding of pure silver for this copy of the Gospels. This I did for the glory of God and by way of thanksgiving, and I keep it constantly on my breast.

I listened to the Captain's story with pleasure and said: "I also happen to know a similar case. There was a workman at our village factory, a nice fellow, very clever at his work. Unfortunately he used to drink, and not infrequently. A certain God-fearing man had suggested that whenever a craving for alcohol gripped him he should recite the Prayer of Jesus thirty-three times for the glory of the Holy Trinity and in remembrance of the thirty-three years of the earthly life of Jesus Christ. The workman paid heed to this advice and carried it out. In a short while he was no longer drinking at all. And what is more, he entered a Monastery three years later."

"Which do you think is best?" asked the captain, "the Prayer of Jesus or the Gospels?"

"It is quite the same thing," I answered. "What the Gospel is, so is the Prayer of Jesus, for the Divine Name of Jesus Christ contains all the truth of the Gospel. The Holy Fathers tell us that the Prayer of Jesus summarizes the whole Gospel."

We set out to say the prayers after our conversation. The Captain started on the Gospel of St. Mark from the beginning. I listened to it and recited the Prayer in my heart. After one o'clock in the morning he finished his reading and we retired to rest.

I got up at day-break as usual, when everybody was still asleep. When it began to dawn I got hold of my beloved *Philokalia*. With what joy I opened it! It was as though I had seen my own father returning from a distant land, or a dead friend who had just risen. I covered it with my kisses, thanking God for having returned it to me. Wasting no time, I opened the second part of the book and began to read Theoliptus of Philadelphia. His instructions startled me, for he suggests that one and the same person do three different things at once. "Seated at the table, give nourishment to your body, fill your ears with reading and your mind with prayer." But when I remembered the happy evening I had spent the day before, I understood from my own experience what was the real meaning of his thought. And here I got the revelation that mind and heart are not one and the same thing.

When the Captain rose I went to bid him farewell and to thank him for his kindness. He treated me to tea, gave me a ruble and said good-bye. Joyfully, I started on my way. I had gone scarcely a *verst*, when I recalled that I had promised to give the soldiers a ruble which had come into my possession in an unexpected way. At first I wondered whether I should give it to them or not. After all, they had beaten me and robbed me; besides, money would be of no use to them since they were under arrest. Then another thought coursed through my mind. I remembered what the Bible says: "If thy enemy be hungry, give him to eat." And Jesus Christ bade us "to love our enemies"; and "if any man will take away thy coat let him have thy cloak also." Thus, the question was settled in my mind. I retraced my steps and came just in time, when the prisoners were about to start on their march. Quickly I approached one of the soldiers and slipped the ruble into his hands, saying: "Repent and pray. Jesus Christ is merciful. He will not forsake you." I left them with these words and went on my way in another direction.

I walked for some fifty *versts* along the high road. Then I decided to take a side-road so as to be alone and read in peace. I was going through a dense forest for a long time. Only rarely did I come upon even small villages. Occasionally I would spend nearly a whole day sitting in the forest and attentively reading the *Philokalia*, which to me was an inexhaustible source of knowledge. There was in my heart a burning desire to unite with God by means of inner prayer, and I was anxious to learn it, using my book as a guide. I could not help regretting that I had no abode where I could read in peace all the time.

Meanwhile I was also reading my Bible and became aware of a clearer understanding of it than before, when I had failed to grasp a multitude of things and had many perplexities. The Holy Fathers were right in their assertion that the *Philokalia* represents a key to the mysteries of the Scripture. It helped me to understand, to a certain degree, the Word of God in its hidden meaning. I began to perceive the significance of the following sayings: "The inner secret man of the heart," "true prayer," "worships in the spirit," "the Kingdom of God within us," "the intercession of the Holy Spirit with unspeakable groanings," "abide in Me," "give Me thy heart," "to put on Christ," "the betrothal of the Spirit to our hearts," the cry from the depths of the heart, "Abba, Father," and so forth. And when I prayed in my heart bearing all this in mind, everything about me appeared to be pleasing and lovely. It was as though the trees, the grass, the birds, the earth, the air and the light were saying that they existed for the sake of man, in testimony and proof of the love of God for mankind. It was as if they were saying that everything prayed and praised God.

In this manner I began to get the meaning of what the *Philokalia* describes as "the understanding of the language of the creation" and I saw that there were ways of conversing with all the creatures of God.

Thus I wandered about for a long time. Finally I came to a district so isolated that for three days I saw no villages at all. My provision of rusk was exhausted, and I was disheartened at the thought that I might perish from hunger. Then I prayed in my heart, entrusting myself to the divine will, and my anxiety left me at once. My mind was at peace again and I regained my good spirits. As I walked farther along the road bordered by a vast forest, a dog ran out of it and trotted in front of me. When I called him, he came up to me in a friendly fashion. I was very happy at the thought that this was another proof of God's mercy. Surely there was a flock grazing in the forest and this dog belonged to the shepherd. There was also a possibility that a hunter was in the neighborhood. At any rate I would be able to ask for bread, if nothing else, for I had gone without food for twenty-four hours. At least they would be able to tell me where the nearest village was.

The dog jumped around me for a while, but seeing that I was not going to give him anything, he ran back to the narrow path by which he had come. I had followed him for a few hundred yards among the trees when I noticed that he ran into a burrow, looked out and barked. And then out from behind a large tree came a middle-aged peasant, gaunt and pale. He wanted to know where I came from. In my turn, I asked him what he was doing there, and a friendly conversation began. The peasant invited me to his hut, explaining that he was a forester in charge of this particular section which had been sold for timber. As he placed bread and salt in front of me, we began to talk once more. "I just envy you," I said. "Aren't you lucky to live here quietly, all by yourself. Look at me, I ramble from place to place and rub shoulders with all kinds of people."

"You may stay here if you wish," he said. "The old dugout of the former forester is not far from here. It is in bad condition, but still good enough to live in in summer. You have your passport. Don't worry about bread; we shall have enough for both of us. My village supplies me with it every week. This little brook here never dries up. This is all I need, brother. For the past ten years I have lived on bread only and drunk nothing but water. That's how it goes. In the fall, when the farmers have finished tilling the land, some two hundred workers will come to fell these trees. Then my business here will come to an end, and you will not be permitted to remain either."

As I heard all this I well-nigh fell to his feet from sheer joy. I knew not how to thank God for His mercy. My greatest desire was fulfilled in this unexpected way. There were still over four months at my disposal before the next fall. And during that time I could give myself to attentive reading of the *Philokalia* in my endeavor to study and to master the unceasing Prayer of the Heart. Thus, I stayed there with joy and lived in the dugout he had shown me.

I often talked with this simple-hearted brother who had sheltered me, and he told me the story of his life and of his thoughts.

"I enjoyed a good position in our village," he said. "I owned a workshop where I dyed red and blue linens. My life was easy but not without sin. I cheated, swore in vain, used foul language, drank to excess and quarreled with my neighbors. There lived in our village an old church reader who had an ancient book on the Last Judgment. He used to go from house to house reading from it and thus earning a few pennies. Occasionally he would come to me. For ten kopecks he would read all night long till cock-crow. While working, I often listened to his reading about the torments of Hell, about the living who will be changed and the dead who will rise from their graves, about God who will judge the world with the angels sounding their trumpets. I learned about fire and pitch and the worms which will eat up sinners. One day as I listened I was overcome by horror at the thought that these torments might be in store for me. Stop! I decided to work for the salvation of my soul, hoping that I would be able to pray my sins away. I pondered over the whole matter, then I quit my work; and since I was all alone in the world, I sold my house and took the job of forester here. All I ask of the village assembly is bread, a few clothes and candles for my prayers. I have lived in this manner for over ten years. I eat once a day and my meal consists of bread and water only. I get up with the roosters, make my morning devotions, burn the seven candles in front of the holy icons and pray. When I make my round in the forest I wear sixty pounds of iron chains under my clothes. I never use bad language, never drink wine or beer and no longer come to blows. As for women and girls, I have been avoiding them all my life.

"At first I was very pleased with my existence, but now other thoughts begin to assail me, and I cannot be rid of them. Only God knows whether I will be able to atone for my sins in this way. And my life is hard. I cannot help wondering if everything written in that book is true. Is it possible for the dead to rise again? And what if a man has been dead for over a hundred years, and even his ashes exist no longer? Who can tell whether there is a Hell or not? Why, no one has returned from the beyond! It seems that when a man dies and rots, he is gone forever. That book might have been written by Priests and lords so as to frighten us poor fools, and keep us quiet. Perhaps we torment ourselves in vain and forsake our pleasures and happiness for nothing at all. What then, if there is no such thing as an after-life? Would it not be better to enjoy what we have on earth and take things easy? I am often disturbed by such thoughts now. I don't know. Maybe some day I shall return to my former work."

I listened to him with compassion. They say, I thought that only educated and intelligent men have no faith whatever. Well, here was one of ourselves, an ordinary peasant, and what impious thoughts he had! It looks as if the kingdom of darkness finds access to everyone, and perhaps the simple-minded are its easiest prey. Let us seek wisdom and strength in the Word of God and brace ourselves for the fight with the enemy of our souls.

It was my sincere desire to help this brother in strengthening his faith. With this intention I took the *Philokalia* out of my knapsack, opened it and read to him the 109th chapter of Saint Hesychius. I tried to explain that it was worthless and vain to keep away from sin merely from fear of Hell and told him that the only way to relieve our souls from sinful thoughts is to guard our mind and purify our hearts by means of inner prayer. The Holy Fathers tell us that those who seek salvation from the mere fear of Hell are regarded as slaves, and those who perform glorious deeds in order to be rewarded with the Kingdom of Heaven are simply mercenary. God wills us to come to him in the manner of sons. He wishes us to lead honorable lives for the love of Him and from the eagerness to serve Him. He wishes us to seek felicity in uniting ourselves to Him in mind and heart.

"However difficult may be the physical tasks which you impose upon your body, it is a wrong way to strive for peace," I said. "Without God in your mind and the unceasing Prayer of Jesus in your heart, you are almost certain to slip back into sin on the slightest provocation. Start to work, brother, make up your mind to say the Jesus Prayer unceasingly. You have here, in this remote place, a unique opportunity to do it. And you will profit by it in a short time. Godless thoughts will assail you no longer. The faith and the love of Jesus Christ will be revealed to you. You will be given to understand how the dead rise; what the Last Judgment is in reality. You will be amazed at the sense of lightness and bliss that follows the Prayer. Boredom will fade away and will not trouble your solitary life.

Then I began to explain as well as I could how one is to proceed with the unceasing Prayer of Jesus, what is said about it in the Word of God and in the instructions of the Holy Fathers. He seemed to compose himself and to agree with me.

After this we separated and I locked myself in the old dugout he had given me. Almighty God! How happy and calm I was when I crossed the threshold of my cave, which looked more like a tomb. To me it was a splendid royal palace filled with comfort and delight. Shedding tears of joy I offered thanksgiving to God and thought that in this peaceful and quiet place I must start to work at my task and beg God for enlightenment. So, once more I began to read the *Philokalia* from the first page to the end, with great attention. Before long I had finished the entire book and realized how much wisdom, sanctity and profound insight it contained. But it dealt with such a vast variety of subjects and so many instructions of the Holy Fathers that it was beyond me to understand all and to summarize all I wished to know, particularly about inner prayer. Yet I ardently longed for it, in accordance with the divine bidding in the words of the Apostle: "Be zealous for the better gifts," and further, "extinguish not the Spirit." I pondered over it for a long time. What was I to do? The task was beyond my reason and my understanding, and there was no one who could have explained it to me - I resolved to beset the Lord with my Prayer. He could enlighten me somehow or other. And for twenty-four hours I did nothing but pray, without ceasing for a moment. At last my thoughts stilled and I fell asleep.

I dreamt that I was in the cell of my departed elder who was explaining the *Philokalia* to me. He was saying: "There is a deep wisdom in this holy book. It is the hidden treasury of the meanings of the mysterious ways of God. The access to this treasury is not revealed everywhere and to everybody. And the guidance given here is subordinated to individual needs: the wise receives from it a subtle guidance, the plain man a simple one. Therefore you, simple-minded, must not read the chapters in succession as they appear in this book. It was meant for those who are versed in theology. Those who are not thus instructed but wish to learn inner prayer, should read the *Philokalia* in the following order: (1) the book of Nicephorus the Monk (part two must be read first of all); (2) then take the entire book of Gregory of Sinai, leaving out the short chapters; (3) read the Three Forms of Prayer by Simeon the New Theologian and his sermon on Faith; (4) then comes the book of Callistus and Ignatius. These Fathers give full guidance and instruction in the inner Prayer of the Heart, couched in words accessible to everyone. If you desire a still clearer understanding of prayer, open part four and read of the way of prayer as it was summarized by the most holy Callistus, Patriarch of Constantinople."

In my dream, still holding the book in my hand, I was trying to find this particular instruction but failed. Then the elder went through a few pages himself, saying, "Here it is. Let me mark it for you." And with a piece of charcoal picked up from the floor he indicated with a mark on the margin the chapter he had found. I listened to him carefully, trying to remember, word for word, what he had been saying.

It was still dark when I woke up. I lay quietly thinking of my dream and of the words of my elder. "God alone knows," I said to myself, "whether I have really seen the spirit of my departed teacher or only imagined it in my mind, for it is constantly riveted on the *Philokalia* and on him." Prey to this doubt, I rose at daybreak. And behold! The book lay on a stone which I used as a table in my dugout; it was open at the very page which my elder had indicated to me, with the charcoal mark on the margin, just as I had seen it in my dream. And the charcoal lay next to the book. I looked in amazement, for the book had not been there the evening before. On that point my recollection was clear; I had closed it and slipped it under my pillow; neither had there been the charcoal on it. I was quite sure of that, too.

This strengthened me in my belief that my dream was true and that my beloved teacher of blessed memory was agreeable to the Lord. I started to read the *Philokalia* just as he had bidden me to do. I read it once, then again, and my soul was aroused by an ardent longing to experience in practice what I have been reading about. Now I understood clearly the meaning of inner prayer, how it may be attained and what the fruits of it are. I also was given to see how it filled the heart with sweetness and how one was to recognize whether that sweetness came from God, from natural causes, or from delusion.

I began to seek the place of my heart in the manner Simeon the New Theologian taught. With my eyes closed I looked upon it in thought, i.e., in imagination. I tried to see it as it is in the left side of my breast and to listen attentively to its beating. At first I did it several times a day for half an hour, and failed to see anything but darkness. Then I succeeded in picturing my heart and the movement in it, and I learned how to bring in and out of it the Jesus Prayer, timing it with my breathing. In this I followed the teaching of Sts. Gregory of Sinai, Callistus and Ignatius. While inhaling, I saw my heart in my mind and said: "Lord Jesus Christ." In breathing out, I said: "Have mercy on me." This I did for an hour at a time, later for two hours, then as long as I was able to. Finally, I succeeded in doing it almost all day long. If things were hard to manage and I fell prey to laziness and doubt, I hastened to open the *Philokalia* and to read passages dealing with the action of the heart, and then once more I felt a fervent and eager desire for the Prayer.

About three weeks later I noticed that my heart ached. Afterwards this pain was transformed to the delightful sensation of warmth, comfort and peace. This incited me still further and urged me to the saying of the Prayer with greater care. My thoughts dwelt constantly on it and I felt a great joy. From that time on I began to experience occasionally a great many different sensations in my heart and my mind. Now and then my heart would brim over with happiness overwhelmed by such lightness, freedom and solace that I was all changed and enraptured. At times I felt a glowing love for Jesus Christ and all God's creatures; and my eyes filled with tears of gratitude to God, Who poured His grace on me, a great sinner. As for my mind, so dull before, it sometimes received such an enlightenment that I was able to understand easily and to meditate upon things which hitherto had been beyond my comprehension. Now and then a sensation of delightful

The Way of A Pilgrim

warmth would spread from my heart throughout my whole being, and I would be profoundly moved in recognizing God's presence in all things. Again, when I called upon the Name of Jesus I would be overwhelmed with bliss, and the meaning of "The Kingdom of Heaven is within you" would become clear to me.

From these and other, similar, comforting experiences I drew the conclusion that the results of inner prayer are threefold: it manifests itself in the spirit, in feelings and in revelations; the spirit is filled by a mellowness that comes from the love of God, inward calmness, exultation of mind, purity of thoughts and sweet remembrance of God. The feelings convey to us a delightful warmth of the heart, a joyful exultation, lightness and vigor, enjoyment of life and insensibility to pain and sorrow. The revelation brings us enlistment of the mind, understanding of the Holy Scriptures and of the speech of all creatures, freedom from vanities, awareness of the sweetness of the inner life and cognizance of the nearness of God and of His love for mankind.

After having spent some five months in solitude and prayer which filled me with sweet sensations, I grew so used to it that I practiced it constantly. In the end I felt that it was going on by itself in my mind and heart, not only while I was awake but also in my sleep. It never ceased for a single moment in whatever business I might have been doing. My soul gave thanks to God, and my heart melted away in continuous joy.

The time came for the felling of the trees. People began to arrive in great numbers, and I was compelled to leave my silent abode. I thanked the forester, prayed, kissed the plot of land on which God had showed His grace to me, unworthy of His mercy, donned my knapsack and set off. I wandered for a long time in different places until I reached Irkutsk. The self-acting Prayer of the Heart comforted and braced me on my journey. Wherever I found myself, whatever I did, it was never in my way, nor was it hindered by anything at all. When I was working at something with the inner Prayer of the Heart, my business progressed more readily. Whether I was listening to something attentively or reading, the Prayer still went on at the same time. I was cognizant of both things simultaneously, as though my personality had been split and there were two souls in my body. Almighty God! How mysterious is the nature of man. "How manifold are Thy works, O Lord! In wisdom hast Thou made them all."

On my way I met with many adventures and happenings. If I were to relate them I should not finish in twenty-four hours. Here is an example of it! One winter evening I was walking alone through the woods towards a village about two *versts* away, where I was to take a night's rest, when a big wolf sprang at me all of a sudden. I held in my hand the wooden chotki of my elder, which I always carried with me, and made the motion of striking the animal with it. The chotki somehow or other encircled the neck of the wolf and was pulled out of my hand. As he leapt away from me, the wolf caught his hind paws in a thorny bush. Furiously he dashed about but failed to extricate himself, for the chotki, also caught on the branch of a dead tree, was tightening around his neck. I crossed myself in faith and went to set him free, mainly because I feared that if the chotki snapped, he might run off with my precious possession. And sure enough, scarcely had I got hold of the chotki when he broke free and darted away, leaving not a trace. I gave thanks to God and thinking of the elder on my way, I came hale and hearty to the village inn, where I asked for shelter.

At the corner table in the inn two men sat drinking tea. One of them was old, the other middle-aged and stout. They did not look like ordinary folk, and I asked the peasant caring for their horses who they were. He said that the old man was a teacher in the elementary school, and the other a clerk in the district court. Both belonged to the gentry. The peasant was taking them to the fair some twenty *versts* away.

After sitting there for a while I borrowed a needle and thread from a woman, drew closer to the candlelight and began to mend my broken chotki.

The clerk noticed it and said: "You've been praying so hard that you broke your chotki?"

"It was not I who broke it, it was the wolf," I answered.

"What! A wolf? Say, do wolves pray too?" he said humorously.

I told them the whole story and explained why the chotki was so dear to me. The clerk laughed: "To you bigots," he said, "miracles seem always to happen. What is miraculous about all this? The wolf was frightened and ran off simply because you hurled something at him. It is a known fact that wolves and dogs are scared by the gesture of hurling, and getting caught in the thicket is also quite common. Many things happen in the world. Shall we see miracles everywhere?"

The Way of A Pilgrim

Hearing this the schoolteacher shook his head: "Don't say that sir," he replied, "you are not expert in science. As for me, I can readily see in this peasant's story the mystery of nature, which is sensuous and spiritual at the same time."

"How is that?" asked the clerk.

"It is like this. Though you have not received any higher education, you are nevertheless familiar with the sacred history of the Old and New Testaments through the catechetical instructions we use in our schools. Do you remember that when Adam, the first man, still enjoyed the state of holy innocence all animals were obedient to him, approached him in reverence and received their names from him? The elder who owned this chotki was a saint. And what is sanctity? It is the return of the sinner to the innocence of the first man. When the soul is holy, the body too becomes sanctified. This chotki had always been in the possession of a saintly man. Thus the touch of his hands and the emanations of his body had endowed it with the holy power of the first man's innocence. This is a mystery of spiritual nature. Now then: all animals in succession, down to our own times, have experienced this power naturally by means of the sense of smell, for in all animals the nose is the main organ of the senses. This is the mystery of sensuous nature."

"You learned men are always talking about forces and wisdoms. For my part, I take things more simply. Fill your tumbler with vodka and send it down, and you'll have all the force you want," said the clerk, and he went to the cupboard.

"That is your business. As for the learned matters, pray, leave them to us," said the schoolteacher.

I liked the way he talked, so I approached him and said: "May I tell you, sir, a few more things about my elder?"

And I told him how the elder appeared to me in my dream, how he had instructed me, and made the charcoal mark in the *Philokalia*. The schoolteacher listened attentively, but the clerk, who had stretched out on the bench, grumbled: "It is true enough when they say that people go out of their mind from reading the Bible too often. That is what it is! What devil would come up at night to mark your book? You let it drop down yourself in your sleep and got it soiled with soot. There is your miracle. Ah, you cunning old fox! I have come across plenty of your kind!"

Mumbling this, he rolled over to the wall and fell asleep.

At these words, I turned to the schoolteacher and said: "I'll show you, if I may, the very book, which was really marked and not just soiled with soot." I took the *Philokalia* from my knapsack and showed him. "What amazes me," I said, "is how a disembodied spirit could have picked up a piece of charcoal and written with it."

The schoolteacher looked at the mark and began to speak:

"This, too, is a mystery of the spirit. I will explain it to you. You see, when spirits appear in a physical form to a living man, they compose for themselves a palpable body from the air and the particles of light. After their

61

appearance, they return to the elements what they have taken out for the composition of their bodies. And since the air possesses elasticity - a capacity of contraction and expansion - the soul vested in it can take anything and act and write. But let me see your book." He took it and chanced to open at the sermon of St. Simeon the New Theologian. "Ah," he said, "this must be a theological book. I have never seen it before."

"This book, sir, consists almost entirely of instructions on inner prayer in the Name of Jesus Christ. It is revealed here in full detail by twenty-five Holy Fathers," I told him.

"I also know something about inner prayer," said the school teacher.

I bowed before him to the ground and asked him to tell me what he knew of it.

"Well, the New Testament tells us that men and all creation 'are subject to vanity not willingly,' but sigh and long for the liberty of the children of God. This mysterious sighing of all creation, the innate longing of souls for God, is inner prayer. There is no need to learn it, for it is inherent in everything and everyone."

"But how is one to find it, to discover it in one's heart, to take it by one's own will that it may act manifestly, give gladness, light and salvation?" I asked.

"I don't remember whether there is anything concerning this subject in theological treatises," said the schoolteacher.

The Way of A Pilgrim

"Oh, yes, there is. Everything is explained here," I said, pointing at the book.

He took out a pencil, wrote down the title of the *Philokalia* and declared: "I shall most certainly have a copy sent me from Tobolsk, and examine it." After that we separated, and when I started off, I thanked God for this conversation with the schoolteacher. As for the clerk, I prayed that our Lord would cause him to read the *Philokalia*, be it only once, and let him find through it enlightenment and salvation.

Another time, in spring, I came to a village, and it so happened that I stayed in the house of a Priest. He was a kindly man, living quite alone. I spent three days with him. When he had observed me for that length of time, he said: "Stay here; you will be paid. I am looking for a dependable man. We are building a new stone church near the old wooden chapel. I need a trustworthy person to keep an eye on the workmen and stay in the chapel to take care of the collection for the building fund. It is just the sort of thing you can do, and you will suit your way of life perfectly. You will sit alone in the chapel and pray. There is a quiet little room for the watchman there. Do stay, please, at least until the church has been built."

I refused repeatedly, but finally I had to yield to the Priest's urging, and I remained there until fall, taking up my abode in the chapel. In the beginning it seemed to be quiet and suitable for prayer, though a great number of people came to the chapel, particularly on holy days. Some of them came to say their prayers, others to fritter away time and still others with the hope of filching money from the collection plate.

The Way of A Pilgrim

Sometimes I read the Bible and the *Philokalia*; some of the visitors saw this and started a conversation; others asked me to read aloud for them.

After a while I noticed a young peasant girl who came frequently to the chapel and spent a long time in prayer. Giving ear to her mumbling, I discovered that some of the prayers were very strange and the others were completely distorted. I asked her where she had learned them; she said that it was from her mother, who belonged to the church. Her father, however, was connected with a sect that had no Priesthood. I felt sorry for her and advised her to say the prayers correctly, according to the traditions of Holy Church. Then I taught her the right wording of the Lord's Prayer and of the Angelic Salutation, and finally told her: "Say the Prayer of Jesus as often as you can, for it reaches God sooner than any other and will lead you to the salvation of your soul."

The girl heeded my advice and followed it carefully. And what happened? A short while afterwards, she told me that she had grown so accustomed to the Jesus Prayer that she felt an urge to say it all the time. She was filled with gladness and the desire to recite it over and over again. This made me very happy, and I advised her to go on with the Prayer in the Name of Jesus Christ.

Summer was ending. Many of the visitors to the chapel wished to see me, not only for the sake of the reading and advice, but also to tell me all their worldly troubles and even to find out about things they had lost or mislaid. It seemed as though some of them took me for a sorcerer. The girl I had already mentioned also came to me in a state of great distress to ask advice. Her father wanted her to marry, against her will, a man of his sect. The wedding was to be performed not by a Priest, but by a simple peasant. "But this marriage cannot be lawful," cried the girl. "Is it not the same thing as fornication? I will run away some place."

"But where?" I asked. "They will find you anywhere. Nowadays you can hide nowhere without a passport. They'll find you! You had better pray to God fervently to change your father's mind and to safeguard your soul from heresy and sin. This is a much better plan than flight."

As time went on I began to feel that all this noise and confusion were more than I could endure. Finally, at the end of summer, I was determined to leave the chapel and go on with my wanderings as before. I told the Priest of my plans: "You know my condition, Father! I must have peace for my prayers. This place is disturbing and harmful to me. Now that I have shown you my obedience, and stayed here the whole summer, let me go with your blessings on my solitary journey."

The Priest did not wish to let me go. He tried to change my mind: "What hinders you from praying here? Apart from staying in the chapel, you work amounts to nothing, and you have your daily bread. You may say your prayers day and night if you wish, but stay here and live with God, brother. You are of great help to me. You do no go for foolish talk with visitors, you are scrupulous with the collection money, and are a source of profit to the House of God. This is worth more than your solitary prayer. Why do you wish to be always alone? Community prayers are pleasanter. God did not create men to live only to themselves, but to help each other and lead each other on the path of salvation. Think of the saints and the Church Fathers. Day and night they worked hard, cared for the needs of the Church and preached in many places. They didn't sit down in solitude, hiding themselves from people."

"God gives everyone a special gift, Father," I said. "There have been many preachers, but also many hermits. Each has done what he could in his own way and in faith that God Himself was showing him the path of salvation. How do you explain the fact that many of the saints gave up their work as Bishops, Priests, or abbots and retired into the desert to get away from the confusion which comes from living with other people? Thus, St. Isaac the Syrian, who was a Bishop, left his flock; the Venerable Athanasius of Athos abandoned his large Monastery just because their places became a source of temptation to them. For they firmly believed in our Lord's saying: 'What shall it profit a man if he gain the whole world and lose his own soul?'"

"To be sure," said the Priest, "but they were saints!"

"If saints must guard themselves from the hazards of mingling with people, what else can a weak sinner do?" I answered.

In the end I bade farewell to the kindly Priest, who sent me on my way with love in his heart.

Some ten *versts* further on, I stopped in a village for the night. At the inn there was a peasant so gravely ill that I recommended that those who were with him should see that he receive the Holy Mysteries. They agreed with me, and towards the morning they sent for the parish Priest. I remained, for I wished to worship and pray in the Presence of the Holy Gifts. While

The Way of A Pilgrim

waiting for the Priest, I went into the street and sat on the bench there. All of a sudden I saw running towards me from the backyard the girl who used to pray in the chapel.

"What are you doing here?" I asked.

"They have set the day for my betrothal to the sectarian, so I ran away." Then she knelt before me and said: "Have pity on me. Take me along with you and put me in a convent. I do not wish to marry. I wish to live in a convent and recite the Prayer of Jesus. They will listen to you and receive me."

"Look here," I said. "Where do you want me to take you? I don't know a single convent in the vicinity. Without a passport, I can't take you anywhere! No one would receive you. It would be quite impossible for you to hide at a time like this. They will get you at once. You would be sent home and punished as a tramp besides. You had better go home and pray. If you do not want to marry, pretend that you are ill. It is called a saving dissimulation. The holy Mother Clementa did it and so did Saint Marina, when she took refuge in a Monastery of men, and many others."

While we sat there discussing the matter, we saw four peasants driving up the road with a pair of horses. They came straight to us at a gallop, seized the girl and placed her in the cart. One of them drove off with her. The other three tied my hands together and forced me back to the village where I had passed my summer. In answer to all my objections they yelled: "We'll teach you, you fake saint, not to seduce girls."

The Way of A Pilgrim

In the evening I was brought up into the village court. My feet were put in irons and I was left in the prison to await my trial the next morning. The Priest, upon learning that I was in jail, came to see me. He brought me some supper, consoled me and promised to intercede for me as a spiritual father by saying that I was not the kind of man they believed me to be. He sat with me for a while and then left for home.

The district police officer came late in the evening. He was driving through the village on his way somewhere else and put up at the deputy's house. They told him what had happened, and a peasant meeting was called. I was brought again to the village court. We went in and stood there waiting. In came the officer in a tipsy swagger, sat on the table with his cap on and shouted: "Hey, Epiphan! Did the girl, that daughter of yours, swipe anything from your house?"

"No, sir!"

"Has she been caught in doing anything wrong with that blockhead there?"

"No, sir!"

"Very well: this is what our judgment and decision will be. You manage your daughter yourself. As for this fellow, we'll give him a good lesson tomorrow and banish him from the village with strict orders never to return again. That is all."

So saying, the officer got down from the table and went off to bed, while I was put back in prison. Early in the morning two village policemen came, whipped me, and let me go.

I went my way thanking God for having esteemed me worthy to suffer in His Name. This thought consoled me and infused a new glow into my unceasing prayer. None of these incidents touched me very deeply. It was as if I had seen them happen to somebody else, being myself a mere spectator of it all. Even when I was whipped, I had the power to bear it; the Prayer that gladdened my heart made me unaware of anything else.

When I had gone about four *versts*, I met the girl's mother, who was driving from the market with her purchases. She saw me and said that the bridegroom had turned her daughter down. "You see," she added, "he was angry with Akulka for having fled from him." Thereupon, she gave me bread and a pie and I went on.

A long time after this another thing happened. I may tell you about it too. It was the 24th of March--I felt an irresistible desire to make my Communion the following morning, which was the Feast of the Annunciation of Our Lady. I asked for the nearest church and was told that there was one some thirty *versts* away. So I walked the rest of that day and the whole night in order to arrive in time for Matins. The weather was very bad; a cold wind blew strongly; it was snowing and raining in turn. On my way I had to cross a brook; just as I got to the middle, the ice broke under my feet and I fell into the water up to my waist. Drenched as I was, I came to Matins, stood through it and through Divine Liturgy, at which I made my Communion, by the grace of God. As I wished to spend a peaceful day in order to enjoy my spiritual happiness, I asked the warden permission to stay in his guard-room until the following morning. My heart was filled with indescribable happiness and joy. I lay there on the planks in the unheated room, as happy as if I were resting on Abraham's bosom. And the Prayer was surging in my heart. The love of Jesus Christ and His Most Holy Mother swept over me in waves of sweetness and immersed my soul in rapture and delight. At nightfall, however, a sharp pain developed in my legs, and I remembered that they were wet. I paid no attention to it, but listened attentively to the prayer in my heart and was no longer conscious of the discomfort. But in the morning when I tried to get up, I found that I could not move my legs. They were paralyzed and weak as bits of straw. The warden dragged me down off the plank bed. Motionless, I sat in the guard-house for two days. On the third day he began to drive me out saying: "Should you die here, think of the mess I would be in."

I crawled out on my arms with great difficulty and made for the church. There I lay on the steps for another couple of days. The people who passed by paid no attention to me or my pleading. Finally, a peasant came up, sat beside me and talked. After a while he asked, casually: "What will you give me if I cure you? I used to suffer from exactly the same thing, and I know a drug for it."

"I have nothing to give you," I answered.

"What do you have in your bag?"

"Just some rusk and books."

The Way of A Pilgrim

"Well, maybe you'll work for me at least one summer if I cure you?"

"I can't do that either. You see, I can use only one arm, the other is almost completely withered."

"What can you do then?"

"Nothing much, except read and write."

"Ah, you can write! Well then, teach my little boy to write. He can read a little, and I wish him to know how to write. But the masters are dear. They ask twenty rubles to teach him."

I consented to do it. With the help of the warden, he dragged me to his backyard and installed me in an old and empty bathhouse there. Then he began to treat me. He picked from the fields, yards and cesspools all sorts of putrid bones of cattle and birds, washed them carefully, broke them up with a stone and put them in a large earthen vessel. This he covered with a lid having a small perforation in it and placed upside down on an empty jar sunk in the ground. He covered the upper vessel with a thick layer of clay, and put a pile of wood around it which he kept burning for twenty-four hours. "We'll extract some tar from these bones," he said, as he was feeding the fire. The following day, when he raised the jar from the ground, there was in it about a pint of thick, oily, reddish liquid, which dripped through the perforation in the lid of the upper vessel. This liquid had the strong smell of fresh raw meat. The bones in the earthen vessel were no longer black and decayed, but looked white, clean and transparent, like mother of pearl. With this liquid, I rubbed my legs five times a day. And what happened? In twenty-four hours I was able to move my toes. On the third day I could bend and unbend my legs. On the fifth day I stood on my feet and walked through the yard, leaning on a stick. In a word, within a week my legs had become as strong as they were before. I gave thanks to God, musing upon His wisdom and the mysterious power hidden in all creation. Dry, decayed bones, almost completely disintegrated, keep in themselves vital force, color and smell, and can act upon living bodies, communicating life to those which are already half-dead. This is a pledge of the future resurrection of the flesh. I wished that I could point this out to the forester with whom I had lived, remembering how uncertain he had been about the resurrection.

Having in this manner recovered from my illness, I began to teach the lad. I wrote out the Jesus Prayer as a sample of calligraphy, and made him copy the words carefully. To teach him was a restful occupation, for during the day he worked for the bailiff of the estate nearby and came to me while the latter slept - that is, from dawn to late Liturgy. The youngster was bright and soon began to write fairly well. When the bailiff found that he could write, he asked who his teacher was.

"A one-armed pilgrim who lives in our old bathhouse," the boy told him. The bailiff, who was a Pole, took interest in me and came to look me up. He found me reading the *Philokalia*, and he started a conversation by asking: "What are you reading?" I showed him the book.

"Ah," he said, "the *Philokalia*! I saw it in the house of our Priest when I lived in Vilna. I was told, however, that it contains all sorts of tricks and artifices for prayer laid down by Greek Monks. It is like those fanatics of

The Way of A Pilgrim

India and Bokhara who sit and inflate themselves trying to get a ticklish sensation in their hearts and in their foolishness take this purely physical reaction for prayer, considering it to be the gift of God. One must pray simply so as to fulfill our duty to God, stand and recite Our Father as Christ taught us. That will put you in the right groove for the whole day, but not the repetition of the same thing over and over again. That, I dare say, might drive you mad and injure your heart besides."

"Don't speak that way about this holy book, my dear sir!" I said. "It was not written by simple Greek Monks, but by great and holy men of ancient times, by men revered by your own church, such as Anthony the Great, Macarius the Great, Mark the Hermit, John Chrysostom and others. The 'heart method' of inner prayer was taken over from them by the Monks of India and Bokhara, who spoiled and distorted it, as my elder told me. In the *Philokalia*, however, all of the instructions concerning the action of the Prayer in the heart have been taken from the Word of God, from the Holy Bible in which the same Jesus Christ who commanded us to recite the Our Father taught also the unceasing Prayer of the Heart. He said: 'Thou shalt love the Lord thy God with all thy heart and with all thy mind'; 'Watch and pray'; 'Abide in Me and I in you.' And the Holy Fathers, referring to the holy words of the Psalms, 'O taste, and see that the Lord is sweet,' explain this passage in the following way: 'A Christian must seek and find, by every possible means, delight in prayer. He must look constantly for consolation in it and not be satisfied by merely saying "Our Father" once a day.' Now let me read to you how they censure those who do not try to find the happiness of the Prayer of the Heart. The wrong of such is threefold: (1) because they contradict the Scripture inspired by God; (2) because they do not

73

The Way of A Pilgrim

strive for the higher and more perfect state of the soul, but are satisfied with outward virtues, and neither hunger nor thirst for truth, thus depriving themselves of blessedness and joy in the Lord; (3) because, in constantly thinking of themselves and their outward virtues, they often lapse into temptation or pride and thus fall into danger."

"What you are reading," said the bailiff, "is too lofty for us worldly people; it is hard to grasp."

"Well, let me read you something easier about men of goodwill, who, though they lived in the world, had learned how to pray unceasingly." I found in the *Philokalia* the sermon by Simeon the New Theologian on the youth George and read it to him.

The bailiff was very pleased and said: "Lend me this book for a while. I will read it some day at my leisure."

"I may give it to you for twenty-four hours, but not for longer," I answered, "for I read it every day myself and can't live without it."

"Well, then, at least copy out for me what you have just read. I'll pay you."

"I don't want you to pay me. I will make a copy for you in brotherly love, and in hope that God will grant you a desire for prayer."

It was with pleasure that I copied for him the sermon at once. He read it to his wife and they both liked it. Thus it came to pass that they would send for me now and then, and I would take the *Philokalia* and read to them while they sat drinking tea and listening. One day they kept me for dinner. The bailiff's wife, a kindly old lady, sat with us at the table and ate fried fish. By some mishap, she swallowed a bone, which got stuck in her throat, and all our efforts to relieve her failed. She suffered a great ache, and in an hour or so was compelled to lie down. They sent for a doctor who lived thirty *versts* away. In the evening, feeling very sorry for her, I went home.

While I was sleeping lightly that night, I heard the voice of my elder. I did not see him but heard him speak to me. "Your landlord cured you; why, then, don't you try to cure the bailiff's wife? God has bidden us to feel pity for our neighbors."

"I would have helped her gladly, but how? I do not know!" I answered.

"Well, what you must do is this: from her early youth she had an aversion for olive oil, not only when she tastes it, but even its smell makes her very ill. Let her drink a spoonful of it. She will be nauseated, the bone will come out, but the oil will have a soothing effect on the sore in her throat and she will recover."

"And how am I to give it to her since she dislikes it so? She won't swallow it."

"Let the bailiff hold her head and pour it in her mouth even though you have to use force."

I woke up, rushed to the bailiff and told him all this in detail.

"Of what use can your oil be now? She is wheezing and delirious, and her neck is swollen. However, we may try, even if it doesn't help. Oil is a harmless medicine."

He poured some into a wine glass and we made her swallow it. Seized with nausea at once, she ejected the bone along with some blood and was greatly relieved. Soon she fell into a profound sleep. In the morning I came to inquire about her health and found her sitting peacefully at the tea table. She marveled with her husband at the way she had been cured. But what surprised them even more was the fact that her dislike of oil that had been told me in a dream was not known to anyone except to themselves. At that time the doctor drove up and the bailiff's wife told him of her experience. For my part, I told him how the peasant had cured my legs. The doctor heard us through and said: "I am not surprised at either of the cases, for the forces of nature operated in both of them. However, I shall take note of it." And he wrote with the pencil in his notebook.

After this the rumor quickly spread throughout the neighborhood that I was a seer, a doctor and a healer. People streamed to me from all parts to consult with me on their affairs and their troubles. They brought me presents, treated me with reverence and pampered me. I endured all this a week. Then, fearing that I might succumb to the temptation of vainglory, I left the place in secrecy at night.

Once more I started on my lonely journey, feeling as light as if a heavy load had been lifted off my shoulders. The Prayer comforted me more than ever, and at times my heart was glowing with boundless love for Jesus Christ. This joyous bubbling seemed to send flows of consolation through my whole body. The mental representation of Jesus Christ was so vivid that when I meditated on the events related in the Gospel, I seemed to see them before my very eyes. Moved to tears of joy, I sometimes felt such happiness in my heart as I have no words to describe.

It happened at times that for three days or more I came upon no human habitations, and in the exaltation of my spirit I felt as though I were all alone on this earth, just one miserable sinner before the merciful and man-loving God. This sense of complete solitude comforted me, and the rapture I experienced in my prayers was much stronger than when I was among many people.

At last I reached Irkutsk. When I had made my prostrations and said my prayers before the relics of St. Innocent, I began to wonder: "Where shall I go now?" I did not care to stay there for a long time, for it was a large and crowded city. I was going along the streets, deep in my thoughts, when a local merchant stopped me and asked: "You are a pilgrim, aren't you? Won't you come to my house?" He took me to his wealthy home and asked me where I came from. I told him all about my beginnings. He listened and said:

"You should go to Jerusalem on a pilgrimage. That place is more sacred than any other site on earth."

"I should be only too happy to do so," I said, "but I haven't the means of going there. I could get along until I reached the sea, but I cannot afford the voyage. It costs a great deal."

The Way of A Pilgrim

"If you wish me to, I can get the money for you. Last year I sent an old man there, one of our townspeople," said the merchant.

I sank to his feet in gratitude. "Listen," he continued, "I'll give you a letter to my son who lives in Odessa. He has business connections with Constantinople and sends his own ships; he will be pleased to arrange your transportation on one of his boats there. One of his agents will book a passage from Constantinople to Jerusalem for you. He will pay; it does not cost much."

When I heard this I was overcome with happiness and thanked my benefactor for his kindness. Even more did I thank God for the fatherly love and care He showed to me, a wretched sinner, who did no good either to himself or to men, but ate in idleness the bread belonging to others.

I stayed with the generous merchant for three days. He wrote me a letter to his son as he had promised. And now, here I am on my way to Odessa with the intention of reaching the Holy City of Jerusalem. Yet, I do not know whether the Lord will permit me to pray in reverence at His life-giving tomb.

Chapter III

Just before leaving Irkutsk I called on my spiritual father with whom I had had so many talks, and said to him: "Now, that I am ready to go to Jerusalem, I have come to take leave of you and to thank you for your love for me in Christ, unworthy wanderer that I am."

"May God bless your journey," answered the Priest. "But tell me about yourself--who you are and where do you come from? About your travels I have already heard a great deal. Now, I should like to know more about your life before you became a pilgrim."

"Well, I'll gladly tell you about that also. It is not a long story," I answered.

I was born in a village in the province of Orel. After our parents died, there were just the two of us left, my elder brother and I. He was ten years old and I was two. We were adopted by my grandfather, an honorable man, quite well-off. He kept an inn on the main road, and because of his kindness many people stayed in his place. My brother, who was a high-spirited boy, spent most of his time in the village. I preferred to stay near my grandfather. On Sundays and holy days we would go to church together, and at home my grandfather would read the Bible - this very Bible I carry with me now. My brother grew up and turned bad. He began to drink.

Once, when I was seven years old and we were both lying in bed, he pushed me down; I fell and injured my left arm. Never since have I been able to use it; it's all withered up.

The Way of A Pilgrim

My grandfather, seeing that I should never be able to work in the fields, taught me to read from this Bible, for we had no spelling book. He pointed at the letters, made me learn them and form the words. I can hardly understand it myself, but somehow or other by repeating things over and over again, I learned to read after a while. Later, when his eyesight grew weak, he often bade me read the Bible to him, and corrected me as he listened. A certain village clerk often put up at our inn. He wrote a beautiful hand. I watched him write and liked it. Then I began to copy words at his direction. He gave me paper and ink and quill pens. Thus I learned to write. My grandfather was very pleased and admonished me: "God has given you the knowledge of reading and writing, which will make a man of you. Give thanks to the Lord and pray often."

We used to attend all the services at church, and at home said our prayers frequently. I was always made to read the Fiftieth Psalm[4], and while I did so, grandfather and grandmother knelt or made their prostrations.

My grandmother died when I was seventeen years old. After a while my grandfather told me: "There is no longer a mistress in this house, and that is not right. Your brother is good for nothing, and I am going to look for a wife for you." I refused, saying that I was a cripple, by my grandfather insisted, and I got married. My wife was a quiet and good girl about twenty years old. A year later my grandfather fell hopelessly ill. Feeling that death was near, he called me, bade me farewell, and said:

---

[4] This is according to the numeration of the Septuagint, which is the version of the Holy Scriptures used by the ancient Christian Church, and still used by the Orthodox Church today. The King James version of the Bible refers to this as Psalm 51.

The Way of A Pilgrim

"My house and all I have is yours. Live according to your conscience; deceive no one, and above all, pray, for everything comes from God. Trust in Him only. Go to church regularly, read your Bible and remember your grandmother and me in your prayers. Here, take this money. There are a thousand rubles here; be thrifty, do not waste it, but don't be stingy either; give to the poor and to God's church." Soon after this he died and I buried him.

My brother begrudged me the property, which was left entirely to me. He grew more and more angry, and the Enemy incited him against me to such an extent that he even planned to do away with me. Finally, this is what he did one night while we slept and no guests stayed in the inn. He broke into the store-room where the money was kept, took it from the chest and set fire to the store-room. The flames spread rapidly through the whole house before we were aware of them, and we barely escaped with our lives by jumping from the window in our night-clothes. The Bible was lying under our pillow. We grabbed it, and took it with us. As we looked at our burning home, we said to one another: "Thank God, we saved the Bible. This, at least, is a comfort in our misfortune."

Thus, all we possessed burned to ashes, and my brother had disappeared without a trace. Later on we learned that while on a spree, he was heard to boast that he had stolen the money and set fire to the house.

We were left naked and bare-foot, like beggars. With some money we borrowed, we built a little hut and set out to lead the life of landless peasants. My wife was a nimble-fingered person. She knew how to knit, spin and sew. People gave her work; she toiled day and night and

supported me. For my part, I was not even able to make
bast shoes. My crippled arm made me quite useless.
And while my wife was knitting or spinning, I would sit
next to her and read the Bible. She would listen to me,
but sometimes she would begin to weep. When I asked
her: "Why are you weeping? We are still alive, thank
God!" she would answer: "It is that beautiful writing in
the Bible. It moves me so deeply!"

Remembering my grandfather's bidding, we fasted
often, said the Akathist[5] to Our Lady every morning,
and at night made a thousand prostrations to keep away
from temptation. In this manner we lived for two years
in peace. But this is what is really astonishing; although
we had no idea of the inner, heart-acted prayer, but
prayed with our lips only and made senseless
prostrations, turning somersaults like fools, we
nevertheless felt the desire for prayer, and the long ones
we recited without understanding did not seem tiring;
quite the contrary - we enjoyed them a great deal. It
must be true, as a certain teacher once told me, that
secret prayer is hidden deeply in the heart of man,
though he may not know about it. Yet, it acts
mysteriously within his soul and prompts him to pray
according to his power and knowledge.

After two years of that kind of life, my wife suddenly
fell ill with a high fever. She received Communion and
passed away on the ninth day of her illness. Now I was
left completely alone. Unable to work, I was compelled
to beg, though I was ashamed of it. Besides, I was grief-
stricken at the loss of my wife and did not know what to
do with myself. If I happened to enter our hut and see

---

[5] Akathist. One of the many forms of the liturgical hymnody of the
Orthodox Church. Its characteristic is praise. There are Akathists to
Our Lord, to the Mother of God, and to the Saints.

her dress, or maybe a kerchief, I would cry out or even
faint away. Life at home was beyond my endurance.
Therefore I sold my hut for twenty rubles and gave to
the poor whatever clothes my wife and I had possessed.
Because of my withered arm, I was given a passport
which exempted me for good from public duties. And
taking my beloved Bible I left, neither caring nor even
knowing where I was going. But after I had set off I
began to wonder where I should go. "First of all," I said
to myself, "I will go to Kiev. There I will pray at the
shrines of saints and ask for relief in my sorrow." As
soon as my decision was made, I began to feel better,
and reached Kiev greatly comforted. Since then, for the
last thirteen years I have been going from place to place.
I have visited many churches and Monasteries, but now
I prefer to wander in the steppes and the fields. I don't
know whether God will let me go to Jerusalem. There,
if it is His Divine Will, it is high time for my sinful
bones to be laid to rest.

"And how old are you now?"

"I am thirty-three years of age."

"The age of our Lord Jesus Christ."

Chapter IV

"The Russian Proverb is true, which says that 'man proposes but God disposes,'" said I, as I came back again to my spiritual father. "I thought that by now I should certainly be on my way to Jerusalem. But see how differently things have fallen out. Something quite unlooked-for has happened and kept me in the same place here for another three days. And I could not help coming to tell you about it and to ask your advice in making up my mind about the matter.

"It happened like this. I had said good-bye to everybody, and with God's help started on my way. I had gotten as far as the outskirts of the town when I saw a man I knew standing at the door of the very last house. He was at one time a pilgrim like me, but I had not seen him for about three years. We greeted one another and he asked me where I was going.

'God willing' I answered, I want to go to Jerusalem.'

'Thank God! There is a nice fellow-traveler for you,' he said.

'God be with you, and with him too,' said I, 'but surely you know that it is never my way to travel with other people. I always wander about alone.'

'Yes, but listen. I feel sure that this one is just your sort; you will suit each other down to the ground. Now look here, the father of the master of this house, where I have been taken on as a servant, is going under a vow to Jerusalem, and you will easily get used to each other. He belongs to this town, he's a good old man, and what's more he is quite deaf. So much so that however much you shout, he can't hear a word. If you want to ask him anything you have to write it on a bit of paper, and then he answers. So you see he won't bore you on the road; he won't speak to you; even at home here he grows more and more silent. On the other hand you will be a great help to him on the way. His son is giving him a horse and cart, which he will take as far as Odessa and then sell there. The old man wants to go on foot, but the horse is going as well because he has a bit of luggage, and some things he is taking to the Lord's tomb. And you can put your knapsack in with them too, of course. Now just think, how can we possibly send an old deaf man off with a horse, all by himself on such a long journey. They have searched and searched for somebody to take him, but they all want to be paid such a lot; besides, there's a risk in sending him with someone we don't know for he has money and belongings with him. Say "Yes," brother, it will really be all right; make up your mind now for the glory of God and the love of your neighbor. I will vouch for you to his people, and they will be too pleased for words; they are kindly folk and very fond of me. I've been working for them for two years now.'

"All this talk had taken place at the door, and he now took me into the house. The head of the household was there, and I saw clearly that they were quite a worthy and decent family. So I agreed to the plan. So now we have arranged to start, with God's blessing, after attending the Liturgy, two days after Christmas. What unexpected things we meet with on life's journey! Yet all the while, God and His Holy Providence guide our actions and overrule our plans, as it is written, 'It is God which worketh in you both to will and to do.'"

The Way of A Pilgrim

On hearing all this, my spiritual father said, "I rejoice with all my heart, dear brother, that God has so ordered it that I should see you again, so unexpectedly and so soon. And since you now have time, I want, in all love, to keep you a little longer, and you shall tell me more about the instructive experiences you have met with in the course of your long pilgrimages. I have already listened with great pleasure and interest to what you told me before."

"Tell me more about the edifying experiences you have encountered in your wanderings," said my spiritual Father. "It was with great pleasure and interest that I listened to what you told me before."

"I shall do it gladly," I answered, "for I have lived through many things, good and bad. But it would take a long time to tell of them all; besides, I have already forgotten a great deal; I have always tried to remember only that which guided and urged my indolent soul to prayer. All the rest I remember but rarely. Or rather, I try to forget the past, as the Apostle Paul bids us. My late elder of blessed memory also used to say that forces opposed to the Prayer in the heart assail us from two sides, from the right hand and the left. In other words, if the enemy cannot distract us from prayer by means of vain and sinful thoughts, he brings back edifying reminiscences into our minds, or fills them with beautiful ideas so that he may draw us away from the Prayer--a thing which he cannot bear. This is called 'a theft from the right side,' where the soul, forgetting its intercourse with God, revels in a colloquy with itself or with other created things. Therefore, he taught me to shut myself off from even the most sublime spiritual thoughts whenever I am at prayer. And if at the end of the day I remembered that more time had been given to

The Way of A Pilgrim

lofty ideas and talks than to the essential secret Prayer of the Heart, I was to consider it a sign of spiritual covetousness and immoderation.

"Yet, one cannot forget everything. An impression may have engraved itself so profoundly in one's memory that although it seems to be gone, it comes back in all its clarity even after a long while. Such are, for example, the few days God deemed me worthy to stay with a certain pious family:

One day as I was wandering through the province of Tobolsk, I found myself in a certain district town. My provision of rusk had run low, so I went to one of the houses to ask for some bread for my journey. The owner of the house told me: "Thank God you have come at the right time. My wife has just taken the bread out of the oven. Here you are, take this warm loaf. Remember us in your prayers." I thanked him and was putting the bread into my knapsack when his wife saw it and said: "Your knapsack is pretty worn-out. I'll give you another instead," and she gave me a new and a stout one. I thanked them again from the bottom of my heart and went away. Before leaving the town I asked in a little shop for a bit of salt, and the shopkeeper gave me a small bag of it. I rejoiced in spirit and thanked God for letting me, unworthy as I was, meet such kind people. "Now," I thought, "I have not to worry about food for a whole week and shall sleep in peace. 'Bless the Lord, O my soul!'"

About five *versts* or so from that town, I passed through a poor village where I saw a little wooden church with lovely paintings and ornaments on its facade. I wished to honor the house of God and went up to the porch to pray. On the lawn beside the church, two

87

The Way of A Pilgrim

little children, five or six years old, were playing. They might have been the parish Priest's children, except that they were too well dressed for that. After I had said my prayer, I went away. Scarcely had I gone a dozen steps when I heard them shout: "Dear beggar, dear beggar, stop!" The two mites I had just seen, a boy and a girl, were running after me. I stopped. They came up to me and took me by the hand. "Come with us to Mommy; she likes beggars," they said. "She will give you money for your journey."

"Where is your mommy?" I asked.

"Over there, behind the church, behind that little grove."

They led me to a beautiful garden in the midst of which stood a large manor-house. We went inside. How clean it was, and so beautifully furnished! In ran the lady of the house to greet me. "Welcome, welcome! God sent you to us. Where are you from? Sit down, sit down, dear." She took off my knapsack with her own hands, laid it on the table, and made me a sit in a very soft chair. "Wouldn't you like something to eat, or perhaps some tea? Is there anything I can do for you?"

"I thank you most humbly," I answered, "but my bag is filled with food. As for tea, I do take it occasionally, but in our peasant way I am not used to it. But I shall pray that God may bless you for your kindness to strangers in the true spirit of the Gospel." As I said this I felt a strong urge to retire within myself. Prayer was bubbling in my heart and I needed peace and silence to give an outlet to its rising flame. I also wished to hide from others my sighs and tears, and the movements of my face and lips - these outward signs which follow

Prayer. Therefore I got up and said: "Excuse me, Lady, but I must go now. May the Lord Jesus Christ be with you and your dear little children."

"Oh, no! God forbid that you should go now. I won't let you. My husband will be back in the evening. He is a magistrate in the district court. How delighted he will be to see you."

So I stayed to wait for her husband, and gave her a short account of my journey.

Dinner-time came and we sat down to table. Four other ladies came in, and we began our meal. When we had finished the first course, one of them got up, bowed to the icon and then to us. Then she went out; she returned with the second course and sat down again. Then another of the ladies in the same manner fetched the third course. Seeing this I asked: "May I venture to ask if these ladies are related to you?"

"Yes, indeed! They are my sisters. This is my cook and this is the coachman's wife; that one is the housekeeper; the other is my maid. They are married, all of them. We have no unmarried girls in the house."

The more I heard and saw all this, the more I wondered and thanked God for having brought me to these pious people. The Prayer was working strongly in my heart, and I wished to be alone, so as not to hinder its action. As we rose from the table, I said to the lady: "Surely you will want to rest after dinner, and I am so used to walking that I shall go to the garden for awhile."

"I don't need a rest," said the lady. "Tell me something edifying; I will go to the garden with you. If you go alone the children will give you no peace. The moment they see you, they will not leave you at all. They have such a liking for beggars, brothers of Christ and pilgrims."

There was nothing I could do but go with her. We entered the garden. In order to remain silent myself, I bowed down to the ground before her and said: "Pray, tell me in the Name of our Lord if you have lived that pious life very long. How did you come to it?"

"'I will tell you the whole story if you like,' was the answer. 'You see, my mother was a great-granddaughter of St. Joasaph, whose relics rest at Byelgorod. We had a large town house, one wing of which was rented to a man who was a gentleman but not well off. After a while he died; his wife was left pregnant and herself died in giving birth to a child. The infant was left an orphan and in poverty, and out of pity my mother adopted him. A year later I was born. We grew up together and did lessons together with the same tutors and governesses, and were as used to each other as a real brother and sister. Some while later my father died, and my mother gave up living in town and came with us to live on this estate of hers here. When we grew up, she gave me in marriage to her adopted son, settled this estate on us, and herself took the veil in a convent, where she had a cell built for her. She gave us a mother's blessing, and as her last will and testament she urged us to live as good Christians, to say our prayers fervently, and above all try to fulfill the greatest of God's commandments, that is, the love of one's neighbor, to feed and help our poor brothers in Christ in simplicity and humility, to bring up our children in the fear of the Lord, and to treat our serfs as our brothers. And that is how we have been living here by ourselves for the last ten years now, trying as best we could to carry out mother's last wishes. We have a guesthouse for beggars, and at the present moment there are living in it more than ten crippled and sick people. If you care to, we will go and see them tomorrow."

After we had gone indoors, her husband arrived. When he saw me, he greeted me with kindness. We kissed each other in a Christian and brotherly fashion. Then he led me to his own room, saying: "Come to my study, dear brother; bless my cell." We entered his study. How many books there were! and beautiful icons, too, and the life-giving Cross in full size, with a copy of the Gospels lying nearby. I said my prayer and turned to my host: "This is God's paradise here!" Then I asked what kind of books he had.

"I have a great many religious books," he replied. "Here are the Lives of the Saints for the whole year, the works of Sts. John Chrysostom, Basil the Great and many other theologians and philosophers. I also have many volumes of sermons by famous contemporary preachers. My library cost me five thousand rubles or so."

"Do you have anything on prayer?" I asked.

"Yes," he said, "I like very much to read about prayer. This is the very latest book on that subject written by a Priest of St. Petersburg." He took out the book on the Lord's Prayer, and we began to read it with interest. After a while the lady came in and brought us tea, and the little ones dragged a silver basket full of cakes such as I have never eaten before in my life. The gentleman took the book from me and handed it to his wife, saying: "Now, we'll make her read; she does it very well. And we shall have tea meanwhile." The lady began reading and we listened. As I did so the prayer became active in my heart, and I listened to it. The longer she read, the more intense became my prayer, and it filled me with joy. Suddenly I saw something flickering quickly before my eyes in the air, and I thought that it was my late elder. I gave a start, but tried to hide it and said by way of apology: "Pardon me, I must have dozed off for a moment." Then I felt as if the soul of my elder had penetrated into my own or was giving light to it. There was a sort of light in my mind and a great many thoughts concerning the Prayer came to me in a flash. I crossed myself, trying to drive them away with my will as the lady finished the book and her husband asked me whether I liked it. We began to talk again.

"I liked it very much," I answered, "and 'Our Father' is the most sublime and the most precious of all the written prayers we Christians have, since it was given to us by our Lord Jesus Christ Himself. And the interpretation of the prayer which has just been read is a very good one, but it emphasizes mainly the active phase of Christian life, whereas in my reading of the Holy Fathers I have noticed a stress upon the speculative and mysterious side of it."

"In which of the Holy Fathers' works did you read this?"

"Well, for example, in the works of Maximus the Confessor and of Peter the Damascene as given in the *Philokalia*."

"Can you recall what they say? Do tell us."

The Way of A Pilgrim

"Why, certainly! The very first words of the prayer - 'Our Father who art in Heaven' are interpreted in your book as an appeal to the brotherly love we must feel for each other since we all are children of the same Father - and this is quite true. The Holy Fathers, however, give to them another explanation which is more spiritual and profound. They say that we should lift out mind upwards to the Heavenly Father and remember every moment that we find ourselves in the presence of God.

"The words, 'Hallowed by Thy Name,' are explained in your book in the following manner: we must be careful not to utter the Name of God without reverence, nor use it in false oaths; the Holy Name of God ought to be spoken in devotion but never in vain. Yet the mystical interpreters see here a direct call to inner prayer, so that the Most Holy Name of God may be engraved in the heart and hallowed by the self-acting prayer, and at the same time hallow all the feelings and powers of the soul. The words 'Thy Kingdom come' they interpret as a call to inward serenity, peace and spiritual contentment. Further, your book says that the words: 'give us our daily bread' must be understood as a request for the needs of our physical life, not in superfluousness, of course, but just that which we need for ourselves and for the help of our neighbors. But Maximus the Confessor understands by 'daily bread' the nourishment of the soul with the heavenly bread which is the Word of God and the union of the soul with God by meditation upon Him and praying to Him unceasingly in the heart."

"Ah! This is a great thing. But for lay people the attainment of inner prayer is well-nigh impossible," exclaimed the gentleman. "We may deem ourselves fortunate if God helps us to say our ordinary prayers without laziness."

"Don't think that, father. If it were impossible, or too difficult, God would not have bidden us all to do it. His strength manifests itself in weakness. And the Holy Fathers, rich in experience, show us easier ways to attain to inner prayer. Naturally, to the hermit they point out special and higher methods of procedure. But lay people also find in their writings convenient means which truly lead them to inner prayer."

"I have never read anything about the matter," he said.

"Well, if you wish to hear it, I will read to you from the *Philokalia*," I said, taking out my book. I found in part three, page 48, the treatise of Peter the Damascene and began to read: "One must call upon the Name of God even more often than one takes a breath, at all times, in all places in any kind of work. The Apostle says: 'Pray unceasingly,' that is, he teaches men to remember God always, everywhere and in all situations. Whatever you do, keep in your mind the Maker of all things. When you behold light, remember who gives it to you; when you see heaven and earth and sea and all that they contain, be in awe and give praise to their Creator. When you put on your clothes, remember whose gift they are and give thanks to Him who takes care of your needs. In a word, remember and praise God in all your actions, and then you will be praying unceasingly and your soul will be filled with gladness."

The Way of A Pilgrim

"Now, you see yourself how simple and easy the way of unceasing prayer is," I said. "It is within the reach of everyone who still retains some sort of human feelings."

They were greatly pleased with this. My host embraced me and thanked me again and again. In a while we went to supper and the whole household of men and women sat down to table as before. How reverently quiet and silent they were during the meal! After we finished, all of us, including the children, prayed for a long time. They had me read the Akathist to the Sweetest Jesus. Thereafter, the servants retired and the three of us remained alone. The lady went out of the room for a while and then came back with a pair of stockings and a white shirt which she gave me. I bowed down to the ground before her and said: "I won't take stockings, my dear Lady; we peasants are used to leg-bands." She left again and this time brought one of her old dresses of thin, yellow material and cut it into two leg-bands. Her husband observed: "O, my poor man! his footwear is almost falling apart." In his turn he brought me his large, new overshoes which are worn over the boots. "Go to the next room," he said, "there is nobody there, and you can change your shirt." I did so, and when I returned they made me sit down on a chair to put on my new footwear. He wrapped my feet and legs in the leg-bands, and she put on the shoes. At first I would not let them, but they said: "Sit still and don't protest. Christ washed the feet of His disciples." There was nothing I could do but obey, and I began to weep. And they were weeping, too. After this the lady retired for the night to the children's apartment and her husband took me to the summerhouse in the garden. There we had a long talk, after which we slept for an hour or so till we heard the Matins bells. We got ready and made our way to the church. The lady of the house and her little children had already been there for some time. We attended Matins; Divine Liturgy began soon afterwards. I could not help weeping when I saw the light on the faces of my host and his family as they prayed and knelt in devotion.

After the services, the masters, the Priest, the servants and all the beggars went to the dining room together. There were about forty beggars, some of them crippled and sickly-looking. Among them were children, too. All of us sat down at the table, and the meal was silent and peaceful as usual. Summoning my courage, I whispered to my host: "In convents and Monasteries they read Lives of the Saints during meals. This could be done here. You have a set of volumes of the Lives of the Saints for the whole year round."

My host nodded: "Yes, indeed!" and turning to his wife said: "Let's do that, Masha. It will be most edifying! I will begin to read at the next dinner, then it will be your turn, after you the Reverend Father, and then all the brothers who can read will come next."

The Priest, who had already begun his meal, said: "I'd love to listen. As for reading, with all respect, I should prefer not to. At home I am so busy that I don't know which way to turn from worries and obligations of all kinds. With that host of children and animals I must attend to my day is filled up. There in not time for reading or preparing sermons; I long ago forgot what I learned in the seminary."

Upon hearing this I shuddered, but the lady who was sitting beside me patted me on the hand and said: "Father talks like that out of sheer humility. He always belittles himself, but he is a most kindly and saintly man. He has been a widower for the last twenty years, and now takes care of his grandchildren, besides holding services very often." At these words I remembered the saying of Nicetas Stethatus in the *Philokalia*: "He who attains true prayer and love has no discrimination between things and sees no difference between the righteous man and a sinner, but loves them all and condemns no one, as God makes the sun shine and the rain fall upon both the just and the unjust."

Silence fell again. Opposite me sat a beggar who lived in the guest-house. He was quite blind and the host took care of him. He cut fish for him, handed him a spoon and poured his soup.

As I looked at the beggar closely, I noticed that his mouth was always open and his tongue was moving as though it was trembling. I wondered if he wasn't one of those who recite the Prayer, and I went on observing him. At the end of dinner an old woman fell suddenly ill; it must have been a serious attack, for she groaned from pain. The masters of the house took her into their bedroom and laid her on the bed. The lady remained there to look after her, and while the Priest went to get the Holy Mysteries, our host ordered his carriage and dashed to town to fetch a physician.

I felt as if I were hungry for the Prayer. The urge to pour out my soul was strong, yet I had no privacy and peace for nearly forty-eight hours. There was in my heart something like a flood that was about to burst out and overflow all my limbs. My attempt to hold it back caused me a sharp, though delightful, pain in my heart - a pain that could be soothed and calmed only in prayer and silence. Now it became clear to me why those who truly practice self-acting inner prayer avoid men and flee into the solitude of unknown places. I understood also why the Venerable Hesychius considers even the most spiritual and useful talk to be but idle chatter if it is too prolonged, just as Ephrem the Syrian says: "Good speech is silver, but silence is pure gold."

Musing upon the matter, I went to the guesthouse, where everybody was resting after dinner. I went up to the attic; there I calmed down, rested and prayed.

When the beggars got up, I found the blind man and led him to the kitchen garden; we sat down alone and began to talk. "Pray, tell me for the love of my soul," I said, "do you recite the Prayer of Jesus?"

"Yes, indeed! I have been saying it without ceasing for a long time."

"What do you feel when you do so?"

"Only this, that I cannot live without praying day or night."

"How did God reveal it to you? Tell me about it in detail, dear brother."

"You see, I am a craftsman here. I used to earn my living by tailoring. I journeyed to other provinces, going from village to village and making peasant clothes. It happened that I lived for a long time in one village in the home of a peasant for whose family I was working. On some feast day I noticed three books lying by the icons and asked, 'Who is it that can read them?' - 'No one,' I was told. 'These books belonged to our uncle, who was very proficient in reading.' I took out one of these books, opened it at random and read the following words which I remember to this day: 'Unceasing prayer is calling upon the Name of God at all times. Whether one is talking or sitting down, walking, working or eating, or whatever one may be doing, it is meet that one should call on the Name of God in all the places and at all times.' When I read this I thought how easy this would be for me, and I began to do it behind my sewing machine and liked it. People who lived with me noticed it and made fun of me: 'What are you whispering all the time?' they asked. 'Are you a witch-master trying to cast a spell over someone?' I stopped moving my lips so as to hide what I was doing and continued saying the Prayer with the tongue only and grew so accustomed to it that my tongue says it by itself day and night. I went about my business for a long time and then all of a sudden I became completely blind. In my family almost everyone got 'dark water' in the eyes. Because of my poverty our people placed me in the almshouse at Tobolsk - the capital of our province. I am on my way there now, but our hosts have kept me here, for they want to give me a cart to Tobolsk."

"What was the title of the book you read? Wasn't it called the *Philokalia*?"

"Frankly I couldn't tell. I did not look at the title page."

I brought my *Philokalia* and found in part four those very words of the Patriarch Callistus which the blind man recited by heart, and read them to him.

"Why! these are exactly the same words," he exclaimed. "Go on with your reading, brother. Isn't it wonderful!"

The Way of A Pilgrim

When I came to the line that "one must pray with the heart," he asked me with surprise: "What does it mean? How can this be done?"

I told him that a complete instruction on the prayer of heart was given in the same book, called the *Philokalia*, and he urged me to read it to him.

"Well, this is what we ought to do," I said. "When are you planning to leave for Tobolsk?"

"Right away, if you wish me to."

"All right, then. I am starting on my way tomorrow. We'll go together; I will read you all the passages which deal with Prayer of the Heart, and I will tell you how to find your heart and enter it."

"But how about the cart?" he asked.

"Ah, what do you need the cart for? Tobolsk is not too far, a mere hundred and fifty *versts*. We'll walk by easy stages, all by ourselves, you and I, talking and reading about the Prayer as we go." So, our plans were made.

In the evening our host himself came to call us to supper. After the meal, we told him, the blind man and myself, that we were starting on our journey together. We explained that we did not need a cart, for we wished to read the *Philokalia* with more leisure.

The next morning we took the road after thanking our hosts most warmly for their great kindness and love. Both of them came with us about a *verst* from their house, and then we parted, bidding farewell to each other.

We walked in a leisurely fashion, the blind man and I, doing from ten to fifteen *versts* a day. And the remainder of our time we spent in lonely spots reading the *Philokalia*. When we had finished the required passages, he begged me to show him the means by which the mind may find the heart, and the divine Name of Jesus may be brought into it so that we could pray sweetly with the heart.

"Well," I said, "when you fix your eyes upon your hand or your foot, can't you picture them as clearly as if you were seeing them, although you are blind?"

"Indeed, I can," he answered.

"Then try to imagine your heart in the same way; fix your eyes upon it as if they were looking through your breast; picture it as vividly as you can, and listen attentively to its beating. When you have grown used to it, begin to time the words of the prayer with the beats of your heart. Thus, say or think, 'Lord' with the first beat, 'Jesus' with the second, 'Christ' with the third, 'have mercy' with the fourth and 'on me' with the fifth. Repeat it over and over again. This you can do easily, for you have already made the preparation and the beginning of the Prayer of the Heart. Later, you must learn how to bring in and out of your heart the whole Prayer of Jesus, timing it with your breathing, as the Fathers taught. While inhaling, say, or imagine that you are saying. 'Lord Jesus Christ', and, as you breathe out, 'have mercy on me.' Repeat it as often as you can; in a short while your heart will hurt you, but in a light and pleasant way: and the feeling of warmth will spread throughout your whole body. However, beware of imagination! Don't let yourself be lured by visions of any kind. Ward them off, for the Holy Fathers bid urgently that the inner prayer should remain free from visions, lest we fall into delusions."

My blind friend listened to all this carefully and started at once to do what I had told him. At night-fall, when we stopped for a rest, he devoted himself to this practice for a long time. In about five days he began to feel in his heart a delightful warmth as well as a joy beyond words and a longing for unceasing prayer which stirred up in him the love for Jesus Christ. At certain times he saw light, though he could not discern objects. At other times, it seemed to him, when he entered the region of his heart, as though the flame of a burning candle flared up brightly in his bosom, and rushing outwards through his throat, filled him with light. And in this light he could see distant events, as it happened on one occasion when we were going through the forest. He was silent, wholly absorbed in the Prayer. "What a pity," he cried all of a sudden. "The church is on fire and the tower has just collapsed."

"Stop imagining things," I said to him. "This is a temptation to you - nothing but idle fancies which must be put aside. How can anyone see what is happening in the city? It is still twelve *versts* away." He obeyed and continued to pray in silence. When we came to the city towards evening, I actually saw there a few burnt houses and the fallen belfry which had been built on wooden piles. There were throngs of people marveling that it had not crushed any one when it fell. As I figured it out, the catastrophe had occurred at exactly the time when the blind man had told me about it.

The Way of A Pilgrim

He turned to me and said: "You told me that this vision of mine was an idle fancy, but now you see that it was not. How can I fail to love and to thank our Lord Jesus Christ who shows His grace even to sinners, the blind and the unlearned? And I thank you, too, for having taught me how to attain the inner activity of the heart."

"Surely, you must love Jesus Christ and thank Him for His mercy," I answered, "but guard yourself from believing that your visions are a direct revelation of grace. They may occur frequently in a perfectly natural order of things. For neither space nor matter can bind the human soul. It cannot only see in darkness, but also things that are a long way off, as well as those which are nearby. Only we fail to develop this spiritual power to its fullest extent. We suppress it within our crude bodies, or crush it beneath the confusion of our muddled thoughts and ideas. But when we begin to concentrate, when we retire within ourselves and become more sensitive and subtle in the mind, then the soul fulfills its purpose and unfolds its highest power. This process is a natural one. I have heard from my departed elder that even people who are not given to prayer, but who are endowed with the kind of power or acquire it in sickness, can see in the darkest room the light flowing from every object and can perceive things in that light. They can even see their own doubles and enter into the thoughts of other people. However, all that comes directly from the grace of God by the Prayer of the Heart is filled with such sweetness and delight that no tongue can describe it, nor can it be compared to anything in the material world. For anything sensual is inferior when compared with the sweet realization of the grace in the heart."

The Way of A Pilgrim

My blind companion listened attentively and became more humble than ever. The Prayer grew stronger and stronger in his heart and filled him with an ineffable delight. With all my soul I rejoiced at all this, and zealously thanked God who judged me worthy to see such a blessed servant of His.

At last we reached Tobolsk. I took him to the almshouse and left him there, bidding him a loving farewell. Then, once more, I set off on my way.

For about a month I went along at leisure, thinking of the way in which pure lives spur us on to follow their examples. I read the *Philokalia* attentively and re-examined everything I had told the devout blind man. His eagerness fired me with zeal, gratitude and love for God, and the Prayer of the Heart filled me with such gladness that I could not imagine a happier person on earth. Often I wondered whether the bliss in the Kingdom of Heaven could be greater and fuller. Not only did I feel happy within my soul, but the outside world, too, appeared delightful to me. Everything I saw aroused in me love and thankfulness to God; people, trees, plants, animals were all my kind, for I saw in all of them the reflection of the Name of Jesus Christ. At times I felt as light as if I were bodiless and floating blissfully in the air. At other times, when I retired within myself, I was able to see my internal organs, and marveled at the wisdom with which the human body is formed. Then again I felt a joy as if I had been made Tsar, and at such moments of rapture I wished that God would let me die soon, so that I might pour out my gratitude at His feet in the realm of the spirits.

It would seem that somehow I took too great a joy in these feelings, or perhaps it was just allowed by God's will, but for some time I felt a sort of quaking and fear in my heart. Was there, I wondered some new misfortune or trouble coming upon me like what had happened after I met the girl again to whom I taught the Prayer of Jesus in the Chapel? A cloud of such thoughts came down upon me, and I remembered the words of the Venerable John Karpathisky, who says that "the master will often submit to humiliation and endure disaster and temptation for the sake of those who have profited by him spiritually."[6] I fought against the gloomy thoughts, and prayed with more earnestness than ever. The Prayer quite put them to flight, and taking heart again I said, "God's will be done, I am ready to suffer whatever Jesus Christ sends me for my wickedness and pride." And those to whom I had lately shown the secret of entry into the heart and interior prayer had even before their meeting with me been made ready by the direct and secret teaching of God.

Calmed by these thoughts, I went on my way again filled with consolation, having the Prayer with me and happier even than I had been before. It rained for a couple of days, and the road was so muddy that I could hardly drag me feet out of the mire. I was walking across the steppe, and in ten miles or so I did not find a single dwelling. At last toward nightfall I came upon one house standing by itself right on the road. Glad I was to see it, and I thought I would ask for a rest and a night's lodging here and see what God sent for the morrow; perhaps the weather would get better. As I drew near, I saw a tipsy old man in a soldier's cloak sitting on the *zavalina*.[7] I greeted him, saying, "Could I

---

[6] That is, in order to help others spiritually, one must submit to disgrace, misfortune and temptation.

[7] *Zavalina*. A bank of earth against the front wall of the house, flat-topped and used as a seat.

perhaps ask someone to give me a night's lodging here?"

"Who else could give it you but me?" he shouted. "I'm master here. This is a post-house, and I'm in charge of it."

"Then will you allow me, sir, to spend the night at your house?"

"Have you got a passport? Give me some legal account of yourself"

I handed him my passport and, holding it in his hands, he again asked, "Where is your passport?"

"You have it in your hands," I answered.

"Well, come into the house," said he.

He put his spectacles on, read the passport through, and said, "All right, that's all in order. Stay the night. I'm a good fellow really. I'll even give you a drink of vodka."

"I don't drink," I answered, "and never have."

"Well, please yourself, I don't care. At any rate have supper with us."

They sat down to table, he and the cook, a young woman who also had been drinking rather freely, and asked me to sit down with them. They quarreled all through supper, hurling reproaches at each other, and in the end came to blows. The man went off into the passage and to his bed in a lumber room, while the cook

The Way of A Pilgrim

began to tidy up and wash the cups and spoons, all the while going on with the abuse of her master. I took a seat, thinking it would be some time before she quieted down. So I asked her where I could sleep, for I was very tired from my journey. "I will make you up a bed," she answered. And she placed another bench against the one under the front window, spread a felt blanket over them, and gave me a pillow. I lay down and shut my eyes as though asleep. For a long while yet the cook bustled about, but at last she tidied up, put out the fire, and was coming over toward me. Suddenly the whole window, which was in a corner at the front of the house—frame glass, and splinters of wood—flew into shivers, which came showering down with a frightful crash. The whole house shook, and from outside the window came a sickening groan, and shouts and noise of struggling. The woman sprang back in terror into the middle of the room and fell in a heap on the floor. I jumped up with my wits all astray, thinking the earth had opened under my feet. And the next thing I saw was two drivers carrying a man into the house so covered with blood that you could not even see his face. And this added still more to my horror. He was a king's messenger who had galloped here to change horses. His driver had not taken the turn into the gateway properly, the carriage pole stove in the window, and as there was a ditch in front of the house, the carriage overturned and the king's messenger was thrown out, cutting his head badly on a sharp post.

He asked for some water and wine to bathe his wound. Then he drank a glass, and cried, "Horses!"

I went up to him and said, "Surely, sir, you won't travel any further with a wound like that?"

The Way of A Pilgrim

"A king's messenger has no time to be ill," he answered, and out he went.

The drivers dragged the senseless cook into a corner near the stove and covered her with a rug, saying, "She was badly scared. She'll come around all right." The master of the house had another glass and went back to bed, and I was left alone. Very soon the woman got up again and began walking across the room from corner to corner in a witless sort of way, and in the end she went out of the house. I felt as though the shock had taken all the strength out of me, and after saying my prayers I dropped asleep for a while before dawn.

In the morning I took leave of the old man and set off again, and as I walked I sent up my prayer with faith and trust and thanks to the Father of all blessings and consolation Who had saved me when I was in such great danger.

Some six years after this happened I was passing a Convent and went into the Church to pray. The kindly Abbess welcomed me in her room after the Liturgy, and had tea served. Suddenly some unexpected guests came to see her, and she went to them, leaving me with some of the Nuns who waited on her in her cell. One of them, who was pouring out tea, and was clearly a humble soul, made me curious enough to ask whether she had been in the Convent long.

"Five years," she answered. "I was out of my mind when they brought me here, and it was here that God had mercy on me. The Mother Abbess kept me to wait on her in her cell and led me to take the veil."

The Way of A Pilgrim

"How came you to go out of your mind?" I asked.

"It was fright," said she. "I used to work at a post-house, and late one night some horses stove in a window. I was so terrified that it drove me out of my mind. For a whole year my relations took me from one Shrine to another, but it was only here that I got cured." When I heard this I rejoiced in spirit and praised God, Who ordains all things in wisdom.

"I was led to experience a great many other things," I said, looking at my spiritual father, "but I should need more than three days and nights to relate to you all that happened. Still, there is one more incident I might relate to you.

One bright summer day I noticed at the side of the road a churchyard - what is usually called pogost - (that is, a cemetery) a church and clergy-houses. The bells were ringing and I went to Divine Liturgy with the people who lived in the neighborhood. Some of them sat down on the ground before they reached the church. Seeing that I was hurrying along, they told me not to rush: "When the service begins, you'll have to stand about for ages. The Liturgy here takes a long time. Our Priest is sickly and slow."

As a matter of fact, the service did last a very long time. The Priest was still young but emaciated and pale; he celebrated slowly but with great devotion, and his sermon at the end of the Divine Liturgy was simple and beautiful. He preached of the way of acquiring the love of God.

After the Divine Liturgy he invited me to his house and had me stay for dinner. I said to him while we sat at the table: "How slowly and reverently you celebrate, Father!"

"Yes, though my parishioners do not seem to like it," he answered. "They grumble, but I can't help it. For I believe that words uttered without inward feeling and attention are useless to myself as well as to others. What really matters is the inner life and intense prayer. But only, a few are concerned with the inner life. The reason is that they do not care about inward enlightenment."

"And how can one attain it?" I asked. "Is it not very difficult?"

"Not in the least," was the reply. "To attain spiritual enlightenment and become a person of serene inner life, you must take one of the texts of the Holy Scripture and meditate upon it for a long time with all your power of concentration and attention. Then the light of true knowledge will be revealed to you. The same thing may be said about the prayer. If you wish it to be pure, right and sweet take up one of the short prayers of few but strong words, and repeat it often and for a long time. Then you will savor prayer."

This instruction of the Priest pleased me greatly. How practical and simple it was, and yet so profound and wise! I thanked God in my mind for showing me so good a pastor of His Church.

When we finished our meal, the Priest said: "Take a rest after dinner while I read my Bible and prepare my sermon for tomorrow." I therefore made my way to the kitchen. There was no one there except a very old woman who crouched in the corner, coughing. I sat down at a small window and took the *Philokalia* out of

The Way of A Pilgrim

my knapsack. As I was reading it quietly to myself, I heard the old woman in the corner unceasingly whispering the Jesus Prayer. Rejoicing at the most Holy Name of our Lord spoken so often, I told her: "What a good thing you do, mother, by saying the Prayer constantly. It is a most Christian and most salutary one!" "Oh, yes!" she answered. "This is the only joy I have left in my life. 'Lord, have mercy on me.'"

"Have you been in the habit of saying this Prayer for very long?"

"Ever since my early youth! How could I live without it, for the Prayer of Jesus saved me from destruction and death."

"How is that? Pray, tell me about it for the glory of God and the blessed power of the Jesus Prayer." I put the *Philokalia* into my knapsack and came closer, ready to listen to her story. She told me thus:

"I was a pretty girl when I was young. My parents were about to give me away in marriage, and on the eve of the wedding my bridegroom came to see us. Suddenly, when he was about a dozen paces from our house, he collapsed and died without regaining his breath. This terrified me so that I refused to marry and made up my mind to live in virginity and prayer. Though I longed for pilgrimages to holy places, I dared not go all by myself, for I was quite young and feared that wicked people might harm me. Then, an old woman pilgrim I knew taught me to recite unceasingly the Prayer of Jesus in all my wanderings. If I did so, she assured me, no misfortune could ever befall me on my journey. I trusted her and, sure enough, I walked even to far-off shrines many times, and never came to grief. My

111

parents gave me money for my travels. As I grew old and my health failed me, the Priest here out of the kindness of the heart, provided me with board and lodging."

I listened to her with joy and did not know how to thank God for this day in which I had learned so much by these edifying examples of the spiritual life. Then, asking the kindly Priest for his blessing, I started off on my way in gladness.

"Then again, not so long ago, as I was making my way here through the Kazan government, I had a chance of learning how the power of prayer in the name of Jesus Christ is shown clearly and strongly even in those who use it without a will to do so, and how saying the Prayer often and for a long time is a sure and rapid way of gaining its blessed fruits. It happened that I was to pass the night at a Tartar village. On reaching it I saw a Russian carriage and coachman outside the window of one of the huts. The horses were being fed nearby. I was glad to see all this and made up my mind to ask for a night's lodging at the same place, thinking that I should at least spend the night with Christians. When I came up to them I asked the coachman where he was going and he answered that his master was going from Kazan to the Crimea. While I was talking with the coachman, his master pulled open the carriage curtains from inside, looked out, and saw me. Then he said, 'I shall stay the night here, too, but I have not gone into the hut; Tartar houses are so uncomfortable. I have decided to spend the night in the carriage.' Then he got out, and as it was a fine evening, we strolled about for a while and talked. He asked me a lot of questions and talked about himself also, and this is what he told me:

The Way of A Pilgrim

"'Until I was sixty-five I was a captain in the navy, but as I grew old I became the victim of gout--an incurable disease. So I retired from the service and lived, almost constantly ill, on a farm of my wife's in the Crimea. She was an impulsive woman of a volatile disposition, and a great cardplayer. She found it boring living with a sick man and left me, going off to our daughter in Kazan, who happened to be married to a civil servant there. My wife laid hands on all she could, and even took the servants with her, leaving me with nobody but an eight-year-old boy, my godson. So I lived alone for about three years. The boy who served me was a sharp little fellow, and capable of doing all the household work. He did my room, heated the stove, cooked the gruel, and got the samovar[8] ready. But at the same time he was extraordinarily mischievous and full of spirits. He was incessantly rushing about and banging and shouting and playing, and up to all sorts of tricks, so that he disturbed me exceedingly. And I, being ill and bored, liked to read spiritual books all the time. I had one splendid book by St. Gregory Palamas, on the Prayer of Jesus. I read it almost continuously, and I used to say the Prayer to some extent. But the boy hindered me, and no threats and no punishment restrained him from indulging in his pranks. At last I hit upon the following method. I made him sit on a bench in my room with me, and bade him say the Prayer of Jesus without stopping. At first this was extraordinarily distasteful to him, and he tried all sorts of ways to avoid it and often fell silent. In order to make him do my bidding, I kept a cane beside me. When he said the Prayer I quietly read my book, or listened to how he was saying it. But let him stop for a moment, and I showed him the cane; the boy began to do my bidding quite

---

[8] Samovar. A sort of urn heated with charcoal to supply hot water for tea.

The Way of A Pilgrim

willingly and eagerly. Further, I observed a complete change in his mischievous character: he became quiet and taciturn and performed his household tasks better than before. I was glad of this and began to allow him more freedom. And what was the result? Well, in the end he got so accustomed to the Prayer that he was saying it almost the whole time, whatever he was doing, and without any compulsion from me at all. When I asked him about it, he answered that he felt an insuperable desire to be saying the Prayer always.

'And what are your feelings while doing so?' I asked him.

'Nothing,' said he, 'only I feel that it's nice to be saying it.'

'How do you mean--nice?'

'I don't know how to put it exactly.'

'Makes you feel cheerful, do you mean?'

'Yes, cheerful.'

'He was twelve years old when the Crimean War broke out, and I went to stay with my daughter at Kazan, taking him with me. Here he lived in the kitchen with the other servants, and this bored him very much. He would come to me with complaints that the others, playing and joking among themselves, bothered him also, and laughed at him and so prevented him saying his Prayer. In the end, after about three months, he came to me and said, 'I am going home. I'm unbearably sick of this place and all the noise.'

The Way of A Pilgrim

'How can you go alone for such a distance and in winter, too?' said I. 'Wait, and when I go I'll take you with me.' Next day my boy had vanished.

'We sent everywhere to look for him but nowhere could he be found. In the end I got a letter from the Crimea, from the people who were on our farm, saying that the boy had been found dead in my empty house on 4 April, which was Easter Monday. He was lying peacefully on the floor of my room with his hands folded on his breast, and in that same thin frock coat that he always went about my house in, and which he was wearing when he went away. And so they buried him in my garden.

'When I heard this news I was absolutely amazed. How had the child reached the farm so quickly? He started on 26 February and he was found on 4 April. Even with God's help you need horses to cover two thousand miles in a month! Why, it is nearly seventy miles a day! And in thin clothes, without a passport, and without a kopeck in his pocket into the bargain! Even supposing that someone may have given him a lift on the way, still that in itself would be a mark of God's special providence and care for him. That boy of mine, mark you, enjoyed the fruits of prayer,' concluded this gentleman, 'and here am I, an old man, still not as far on as he.'

"Later on I said to him, 'it is a splendid book, sir, the one by St. Gregory Palamas, which you said you liked reading. I know it. But it treats rather of the oral Prayer of Jesus. You should read a book called the *Philokalia*. There you will find a full and complete study of how to reach the Spiritual Prayer of Jesus in the mind and heart also, and taste the sweet fruit of it.' At the same time I showed him my *Philokalia*. I saw that he was pleased to have this advice of mine, and he promised that he would get a copy for himself. And in my own mind I dwelt upon the wonderful ways in which the power of God is shown in this prayer. What wisdom and teaching there was in the story I had just heard! The cane taught the Prayer to the boy, and what is more, as a means of consolation it became a help to him. Are not our own sorrows and trials which we meet with on the road of prayer in the same way the rod in God's hand? Why then are we so frightened and troubled when our Heavenly Father in the fullness of His boundless love lets us see them; and when these rods teach us to be more earnest in learning to pray, and lead us on to consolation which is beyond words?"

Having finished these tales, I said to my Spiritual Father: "Forgive me in God's Name; I have already talked too much, and the Holy Fathers call even spiritual talk idle chatter if it is prolonged. It is time for me to meet my fellow-traveler to Jerusalem. Pray for me, a wretched sinner, that God in His mercy may prosper me on my journey."

"With all my soul I wish it, my beloved brother in the Lord," he answered. "May the all-loving grace of God overshadow your way and guide you as the Angel Raphael guided Tobias."

The Pilgrim
Continues His Way

The Pilgrim Continues His Way

Chapter I

The Starets[9]. A year had gone by since I last saw the Pilgrim, when at length a gentle knock on the door and a pleading voice announced the arrival of that devout brother to the hearty welcome which awaited him.

"Come in, dear brother; let us thank God together for blessing your journey and bringing you back."

The Pilgrim. Praise and thanks be to the Father on high for His bounty in all things, which He orders as seems good to Him, and always for the good of us pilgrims and strangers in a strange land. Here am I, a sinner, who left you last year, again by the mercy of God thought worthy to see and hear your joyful welcome. And of course you are waiting to hear from me a full account of the Holy City of God, Jerusalem, for which my soul was longing and toward which my purpose was firmly set. But what we wish is not always carried out, and so it was in my case. And no wonder, for why should I, a wretched sinner, be thought fit to tread that holy ground on which the divine footsteps of our Lord Jesus Christ were printed?

You remember, Father, that I left here last year with a deaf old man as a companion, and that I had a letter from a merchant of Irkutsk to his son at Odessa asking

---

[9] *Starets*, pl. *Startsi*. A Monk distinguished by his great piety, long experience of the spiritual life, and gift for guiding other souls. Layfolk frequently resort to *Startsi* for spiritual counsel. In a Monastery a new member of the community is attached to a Starets, who trains and teaches him.

119

him to send me to Jerusalem. Well, we got to Odessa all right in no very long time. My companion at once booked passage on a ship for Constantinople and set off. I for my part set about finding the merchant's son, by the address on the letter. I soon found his house, but there, to my surprise and sorrow, I learned that my benefactor was no longer alive. He had been dead and buried three weeks before, after a short illness. This made me very much cast down. But still, I trusted in the power of God. The whole household was in mourning, and the widow, who was left with three small children, was in such distress that she wept all the time and several times a day would collapse in grief. Her sorrow was so great that it seemed as though she too would not live long. All the same, in the midst of all this, she met me kindly, though in such a state of affairs she could not send me to Jerusalem. But she asked me to stay with her for a fortnight or so until her father-in-law came to Odessa, as he had promised, to settle the affairs of the bereaved family.

So I stayed. A week passed, a month, then another. But instead of coming, the merchant wrote to say that his own affairs would not allow him to come, and advising that she should pay off the assistants and that all should go to him at Irkutsk at once. So a great bustle and fuss began, and as I saw they were no longer interested in me, I thanked them for their hospitality and said good-bye. Once more I set off wandering about Russia.

I thought and thought. Where was I to go now? In the end I decided that first of all I would go to Kiev, where I had not been for many years. So I set off. Of course I fretted at first because I had not been able to carry out my wish to go to Jerusalem, but I reflected that even

The Pilgrim Continues His Way

this had not happened without the providence of God, and I quieted myself with the hope that God, the lover of men, would take the will for the deed, and would not let my wretched journey be without edification and spiritual value. And so it turned out, for I came across the sort of people who showed me many things that I did not know, and for my salvation brought light to my dark soul. If that necessity had not sent me on this journey, I should not have met those spiritual benefactors of mine.

So by day I walked along with the prayer, and in the evening when I halted for the night I read my *Philokalia*, for the strengthening and stimulating of my soul in its struggle with the unseen enemies of salvation.

On the road about forty-five miles from Odessa I met with an astonishing thing. There was a long train of wagons loaded with goods; there were about thirty of them, and I overtook them. The foremost driver, being the leader, was walking beside his horse, and the others were walking in a group some way from him. The road led past a pond which had a stream running through it, and in which the broken ice of the spring season was whirling about and piling up on the edges with a horrible noise. All of a sudden the leading driver, a young man, stopped his horse, and the whole line of carts behind had to come to a standstill too. The other drivers came running up to him and saw that he had begun to undress. They asked him why he was undressing. He answered that he very much wanted to bathe in the pond. Some of the astonished drivers began to laugh at him, others to scold him, calling him mad, and the eldest there, his own brother, tried to stop him, giving him a push to make him drive on. The other defended himself and had not the least wish to do as he was told. Several of the young drivers started getting water out of the pond in the buckets with which they watered the horses, and for a joke splashed it over the man who wanted to bathe, on his head, or from behind, saying, "There you are; we'll give you a bath." As soon as the water touched his body, he cried out, "Ah, that's good," and sat down on the ground. They went on throwing water over him. Thereupon he soon lay down, and then and there quietly died. They were all in a great fright, having no idea why it had happened. The older ones bustled about, saying that the authorities ought to be told, while the rest came to the conclusion that it was his fate to meet this kind of death.

I stayed with them about an hour and then went on my way. About three and a half miles farther on I saw a village on the high road, and as I came into it I met an old Priest walking along the street. I thought I would tell him about what I had just seen and find out what he thought about it. The Priest took me into his house, and I told him the story and asked him to explain to me the cause of what had taken place.

"I can tell you nothing about it, dear brother, except perhaps this, that there are many wonderful things in nature which our minds cannot understand. This, I think, is so ordered by God in order to show men the rule and providence of God in nature more clearly, through certain cases of unnatural and direct changes in its laws. It happens that I myself was once a witness of a similar case. Near our village there is a very deep and steep-sided ravine, not very wide, but some seventy feet or more in depth. It is quite frightening to look down to the gloomy bottom of it. A sort of footbridge has been built over it. A peasant in my parish, a family man and very respectable, suddenly, for no reason, was taken with an irresistible desire to throw himself from this little bridge into that deep ravine. He fought against the idea and resisted the impulse for a whole week. In the end, he could hold himself back no longer. He got up early, rushed off, and jumped into the abyss. They soon heard his groans and with great difficulty pulled him out of the pit with his legs broken. When he was asked the reason for his fall, he answered that although he was now feeling a great deal of pain, yet he was calm in spirit, that he had carried out the irresistible desire which had worried him so for a whole week, and that he had been ready to risk his life to gratify his wish.

"He was a whole year in the hospital getting better. I used to go to see him and often saw the doctors who were around him. Like you, I wanted to hear from the cause of the affair. With one voice the doctors answered that it was 'frenzy.' When I asked them for a scientific explanation of what that was, and what caused it to attack a man, I could get nothing more out of them, except that this was one of the secrets of nature which were not revealed to science. I for my part observed that if in such a mystery of nature a man were to turn to God in prayer, and also to tell good people about it, then this ungovernable 'frenzy' of theirs would not attain its purpose.

"Truly there is much to be met with in human life of which we can have no clear understanding."

While we were talking it was getting dark, and I stayed the night there. In the morning the mayor sent his secretary to ask the Priest to bury the dead man in the cemetery, and to say that the doctors, after a postmortem, had found no signs whatever of madness, and gave a sudden stroke as the cause of death.

"Look at that now," said the Priest to me, "medical science can give no precise reason for his uncontrollable urge toward the water."

And so I said good-bye to the Priest and went on my way. After I had traveled for several days and was feeling rather done-up, I came to a good-sized commercial town called Byelaya Tserkov. As evening was already coming on, I started to look around for a lodging for the night. In the market I came across a man who looked as though he were a traveler too. He was making inquiries among the shops for the address of a certain person who lived in the place. When he saw me he came up to me and said, "You look as though you are a pilgrim too, so let's go together and find a man by the name of Evreinov[10] who lives in the town. He is a good Christian and keeps a splendid inn, and he welcomes pilgrims. Look, I've got something written down about him." I gladly agreed, and so we soon found his house. Although the host himself was not at home, his wife, a nice old woman, received us very kindly and gave us an out-of-the-way private little garret in the attic to rest in. We settled down and rested for a while.

Then our host came and asked us to have supper with them. During supper we talked--who we were and where we came from--and somehow or other the talk came round to the question of why he was called Evreinov. "I'll tell you an odd thing about that," he said, and began his story.

---

[10] *Evreinov*. Literally the name means "son of a Jew."

The Pilgrim Continues His Way

"You see, it was like this. My father was a Jew. He was born at Shklov, and he hated Christians. From his very earliest years he was preparing to be a rabbi and studied hard at all the Jewish chitchat which was meant to disprove Christianity. One day he happened to be going through a Christian cemetery. He saw a human skull, which must have been taken out of some grave that had been recently disturbed. It had both its jaws, and there were some horrible-looking teeth in them. In a fit of temper he began to jeer at this skull; he spat at it, abused it, and spurned it with his foot. Not content with that, he picked it up and stuck it on a post--as they stick up the bones of animals to drive off greedy birds. After amusing himself in this way, he went home. The following night he had scarcely fallen asleep when suddenly an unknown man appeared to him and violently upbraided him, saying, 'How dare you insult what is left of my poor bones? I am a Christian--but as for you, you are the enemy of Christ.' The vision was repeated several times every night, and he got neither sleep nor rest. Then the same sight started flashing before his eyes during the daytime also, and he would hear the echo of that reproachful voice. As time went on, the vision got more frequent, and in the end he began to feel depressed and frightened and to lose strength. He went to his rabbi, who read prayers and exorcisms over him. But the apparition not only did not cease; it got even more frequent and threatening.

"This state of affairs became known, and, hearing about it, a business friend of his, a Christian, began to advise him to accept the Christian religion, and to urge upon him that apart from that acceptance there was no way of ridding himself of this disturbing apparition of his. But the Jew was loath to take this step. However, in reply he said, 'I would gladly do as you wish, if only I could be free from this tormenting and intolerable apparition.' The Christian was glad to hear this, and persuaded him to send in to the local Bishop a request for Baptism and reception into the Christian Church. The request was written, and the Jew, not very eagerly, signed it. And lo and behold, the very minute that the request was signed, the apparition came to an end and never troubled him again. His joy was unbounded, and entirely at rest in mind, he felt such a burning faith in Jesus Christ that he went straight away to the Bishop, told him the whole story, and expressed a heartfelt desire to be christened. He eagerly and quickly learned the dogmas of the Christian faith, and after his Baptism he came to live in this town. Here he married my mother, a good Christian woman. He led a devout and very comfortable life and he was most generous to the poor. He taught me to be the same and before his death gave me his instructions about this, together with his blessing. There you are--that's why my name is Evreinov."

I listened to this story with reverence and humility, and I thought to myself, "How good and kind our Lord Jesus Christ is, and how great is His love! In what different ways He draws sinners to Himself. With what wisdom He uses things of little importance to lead on to great things. Who could have expected that the mischievous pranks of a Jew with some dead bones would bring him to the true knowledge of Jesus Christ and be the means of leading him to a devout life."

After supper we thanked God and our host and retired to our garret. We did not want to go to bed yet, so we went on talking to each other. My companion told me that he was a merchant of Mogilev, and that he had spent two years in Bessarabia as a novice in one of the

The Pilgrim Continues His Way

Monasteries there, but only with a passport that expired on a fixed date. He was now on his way home to get the consent of the merchant community to his finally entering upon the monastic life. "The Monasteries there satisfy me, their constitution and order, and the strict life of many devout Startsi who live there." He assured me that putting the Bessarabian Monasteries beside the Russian was like comparing heaven with earth. He urged me to do the same.

While we were talking about these things they brought still a third lodger into our room. This was a noncommissioned officer, with the army for the time being, but now going home on leave. We saw that he was tired out with his journey. We said our prayers together and lay down to sleep. We were up early next morning and began to get ready for the road, and we only just wanted to go and thank our host, when suddenly we heard the bells ringing for Matins. The merchant and I began to consider what we would do. How could we start after hearing the bells and without going to Church? It would be better to stay for Matins, say our prayers in Church, and then we should go off more happily. So we decided, and we called the officer. But he said, "What's the point of going to Church while you are on a journey? What good is it to God if we have been? Let's get off home and then say our prayers. You two go if you want. I'm not going. By the time you have stood through Matins I shall be three or four *versts* or so farther on my way, and I want to get home as quickly as possible." To this the merchant said, "Look here, brother, don't you run so far ahead with your schemes until you know what God's plans are!" So we went to Church, and he took the road.

The Pilgrim Continues His Way

We stayed through Matins and the Liturgy too. Then we went back to our garret to get our knapsacks ready for the start, when what do we see but our hostess bringing in the samovar. "Where are you off to?" she says. "You must have a cup of tea--yes, and have dinner with us too. We can't send you away hungry." So we stayed. We had not been sitting at the samovar for half an hour, when all of a sudden our noncommissioned officer comes running in, all out of breath.

"I've come to you in both sorrow and joy."

"What's all this?" we asked him.

This is what he said:

"When I left you and started off, I thought I would look in at the pub to get change for a note, and have a drink at the same time so as to get along better. So I did. I got my change, had my drink, and was off like a bird. When I had gone about two *versts* I had a mind to count the money the fellow at the pub had given me. I sat down by the roadside, took out my pocketbook, and went through it. All serene. Then suddenly it struck me that my passport was not there--only some papers and the money. I was as frightened as if I'd lost my head. I saw in a flash what had happened. Of course I had dropped it when I was settling up at the pub. I must run back. I ran and ran. Another awful idea seized me-- suppose it's not there! That will mean trouble! I rushed up to the man behind the bar and asked him. 'I've not seen it,' he said. And was I downhearted! Well, I searched around and hunted everywhere, wherever I had stood and hung about. And what do you think? I was lucky enough to find my passport. There it was, still folded up and lying on the floor among the straw and litter, all trampled in the dirt. Thank God! I was glad, I can tell you; it was as though a mountain had rolled off my shoulders. Of course it was filthy and coated with mud, enough to get me a clout on the head; still, that doesn't matter. At any rate I can get home and back again with a whole skin. But I came to tell you about it. And what's more, in my fright I've rubbed my foot absolutely raw with running and I can't possibly walk. So I came to ask for some grease to bandage it up with."

"There you are, brother," the merchant began, "that's because you wouldn't listen and come with us to Church. You wanted to get a long way ahead of us, and, on the contrary, here you are back again, and lame into the bargain. I told you not to run so far ahead with your schemes; and now see how it has turned out. It was a small thing that you did not come to Church, but besides that you used such language as, 'What good does it do God if we pray?' That, brother, was bad. Of course, God does not need our sinful prayers, but still, in His love for us He likes us to pray. And it is not only that holy prayer which the Holy Spirit Himself helps us to offer and arouses in us that is pleasing to Him, for He asks that of us when He says 'Abide in Me, and I in you'; but every intention, every impulse, even every thought which is directed to His glory and our salvation is of value in His sight. For all these the boundless loving kindness of God gives bountiful rewards. The love of God gives grace a thousandfold more than human actions deserve. If you give Him the merest mite, He will pay you back with gold. If you but purpose to go to the Father, He will come out to meet you. You say but a word, short and unfeeling--'Receive me, have mercy on me'--and He falls on your neck and kisses you. That is what the love of the heavenly Father is like toward us, unworthy as we are. And simply because of this love He rejoices in every gesture we make toward salvation, however small. It looks like this to you: What glory is there for God, what advantage for you, if you pray a little and then your thoughts wander again, or if you do some small good deed, such as reading a prayer, making five or ten prostrations, or giving a heartfelt sigh and calling upon the Name of Jesus, or attending to some good thought, or setting yourself to some spiritual reading, or abstaining from some food, or bearing an affront in silence--all that seems to you not enough for your full salvation and a fruitless thing to do. No! None of these small acts is in vain; it will be taken into account by the all-seeing eye of God and receive a hundredfold reward, not only in eternity, but in this life. St. John Chrysostom asserts this. 'No good of any sort,' he says, 'however trifling it may be, will be scorned by the righteous Judge. If sins are searched out in such detail that we shall give an answer for words and desires and thoughts, then so much the more good deeds, however small they are, will be taken into account in all detail, and will be reckoned to our advantage before our Judge, who is full of love.'

"I will tell you a case which I saw myself last year. In the Bessarabian Monastery where I lived there was a Starets, a Monk of good life. One day a temptation beset him. He felt a great longing for some dried fish. And as it was impossible to get any in the Monastery at that time, he was planning to go to the market and buy some. For a long while he struggled against the idea, and reasoned with himself that a Monk ought to be content with the ordinary food provided for the brothers and by all means to avoid self-indulgence. Moreover, to walk about the market among crowds of people was also for a Monk a source of temptation, and unseemly. In the end the lies of the enemy got the upper hand of his reasoning and he, yielding to his self-will, made up his mind and went for the fish. After he had left the building and was going along the street, he noticed that his chotki was not in his hand, and he began to think, 'Why is it, that I am going like a soldier without his sword? This is most unseemly. And layfolk who meet me will criticize me and fall into temptation, seeing a Monk without his chotki'! He was going back to get it, but, feeling in his pocket, he found it there. He pulled it out, crossed himself, and with his chotki in his hand went calmly on. As he got near the market he saw a horse standing by a shop with a great cartload of enormous tubs. All at once this horse, taking fright at something or other, bolted with all its might and with thundering hoofs made straight for him, grazing his shoulder and throwing him to the ground, though not hurting him very much. Then, a couple of paces from him, that load toppled over and the cart was smashed to splinters. Getting up quickly, naturally he was frightened enough, but at the same time he marveled how God had saved his life, for if the load had fallen a split second earlier, then he would have been smashed to pieces like the cart. Thinking no further about it, he bought the fish, went back, ate it, said his prayers, and lay down to sleep.

"He slept lightly, and in his sleep a benign-looking Starets whom he did not know appeared to him, and said, 'Listen, I am the protector of this dwelling, and I wish to teach you so that you will understand and remember the lesson now given you. Look now: The feeble effort you made against the feeling of pleasure, and your sloth in self-understanding and self-control, gave the enemy his chance to attack you. He had got ready for you that fatal bombshell which exploded before your eyes. But your guardian angel foresaw this and put into your mind the thought of offering a prayer and remembering your chotki. Since you listened to this suggestion, obeyed, and put it into action, it was just this that saved you from death. Do you see God's love for men, and His bountiful reward of even a slight turning toward Him?' Saying this, the visionary Starets quickly left the cell. The Monk bowed down at his feet, and in doing so woke up, to find himself, not on his bed, but kneeling prostate at the threshold of the door. He told the story of this vision for the spiritual benefit of many people, myself among them.

"Truly boundless is the love of God for us sinners. Is it not marvelous that so small an action--yes, just taking his chotki out of his pocket and carrying it in his hand and calling once upon the Name of God--should give a man his life, and that in the scales of judgment upon men one short moment of calling upon Jesus Christ should outweigh many hours of sloth? In truth, here is the repayment of the tiny mite with gold. Do you see, brother, how powerful prayer is and how mighty the Name of Jesus when we call upon it? St. John Karpathisky in the *Philokalia* says that when in the Prayer of Jesus we call upon the holy Name and say, 'Have mercy on me, a sinner,' then to every such petition the voice of God answers in secret, 'Son, thy sins be forgiven thee.' And he goes on to say that when we say the prayer there is at that moment nothing to distinguish us from the Saints, Confessors, and Martyrs. For, as St. Chrysostom says, 'Prayer, although we are full of sin when we utter it, immediately cleanses us. God's loving-kindness to us is great, yet we sinners are listless, are not willing to give even one small hour to God in thanksgiving, and barter the time of prayer, which is more important than anything, for the bustle and cares of living, forgetting God and our duty. For that reason we often meet with misfortunes and calamities, yet even these the all-loving providence of God uses for our instruction and to turn our hearts to Him.'"

When the merchant came to the end of his talk to the officer, I said to him, "What comfort you have brought to my sinful soul too, your honor! I could bow down to your very feet." Hearing this, he began to speak to me. "Ah, it seems you are a lover of religious stories. Wait a moment and I'll read you another like the one I have just told him. I've got here a book I travel with called Agapia, or The Salvation of Sinners. There are a lot of wonderful things in it."

He took the book out of his pocket and started reading a most beautiful story about one Agathonik, a devout man who from his childhood had been taught by pious parents to say every single day before the icon of the Mother of God the prayer which begins "Rejoice, O Virgin Theotokos." And this he always did. Later, when he had grown up and started life on his own, he got absorbed in the cares and fuss of life and said the prayer but rarely, and finally gave it up altogether.

One day he gave a pilgrim a lodging for the night, who told him he was a hermit from the Thebaid and that he had seen a vision in which he was told to go to Agathonik and rebuke him for having given up the prayer to the Mother of God. Agathonik said the reason was that he had said the prayer for many years without seeing any result whatever. Then the hermit said to him, "Remember, blind and thankless one, how many times this prayer has helped you and saved you from disaster. Remember how in your youth you were wonderfully saved from drowning? Do you not recall that an

The Pilgrim Continues His Way

epidemic of infectious disease carried off many of your friends to the grave, but you remained in health? Do you remember, when you were driving with a friend, you both fell out of the cart; he broke his leg, but you were unhurt? Do you not know that a young man of your acquaintance who used to be well and strong is now lying weak and ill, whereas you are in good health and feel no pain?" And he reminded Agathonik of many other things. In the end he said, "Know this, that all those troubles were warded off from you by the protection of the Most Holy Mother of God because of that short prayer, by which you lifted up your heart every day into union with God. Take care now, go on with it, and do not give up praising the Queen of Heaven lest she should forsake you."

When he had finished reading, they called us to dinner, and afterward, feeling our strength renewed, we thanked our host and took the road. We parted, and each went his own way as seemed best to him.

After that I walked on for about five days, cheered by the memory of the stories I had heard from the good merchant in Byelaya Tserkov, and I began to get near to Kiev. All at once and for no reason at all I began to feel dull and heavy, and my thoughts got gloomy and dispirited. The prayer went with difficulty and a sort of indolence came over me. So, seeing a wood with a thick undergrowth of bushes by the side of the road, I went into it to rest a bit, looking for some out-of-the-way place where I could sit under a bush and read my *Philokalia*, and so arouse my feeble spirit and comfort my faint-heartedness. I found a quiet place and began to read St. John Cassian the Roman in the fourth part of the *Philokalia*—on the eight thoughts. When I had been reading happily for about half an hour, quite unexpectedly I noticed the figure of a man some hundred yards or so away from me and farther in the forest. He was kneeling quite motionless. I was glad to see this, for I gathered, of course, that he was praying, and I began to read again. I went on reading for an hour or more and then glanced up again. The man was still kneeling there and never stirred. All this moved me very much and I thought, "What devout servants of God there are!"

As I was turning it over in my mind, the man suddenly fell to the ground and lay still. This startled me, and as I had not seen his face, for he had been kneeling with his back to me, I felt curious to go and see who he was. When I got to him I found him in a light sleep. He was a country lad, a young fellow of about twenty-five. He had an attractive face, good-looking, but pale. He was dressed in a peasant's caftan with a bast rope for a girdle. There was nothing else to note about him. He had no kotomka[11], not even a stick. The sound of my approach awoke him, and he got up. I asked him who he was, and he told me he was a state peasant of the Smolensk government and that he was on his way from Kiev. "And where are you going to now?" I asked.

"I don't know myself where God will lead me," he answered.

"It is long since you left home?"

"Yes, over four years."

---

[11] *Kotomka.* A sort of knapsack made of birch bark. It has two pockets, one in front and another behind, and is worn slung over the shoulder.

The Pilgrim Continues His Way

"And where have you been living all that time?"

"I have been going from shrine to shrine and to Monasteries and churches. There was no point in staying at home. I'm an orphan and I have no relations. Besides, I've got a lame foot. So I'm roaming about the wide world."

"Some God-fearing person, it seems, has taught you not just to roam anywhere, but to visit holy places," said I.

"Well, you see," he answered, "having no father or mother, I used to go about as a boy with the shepherds of our village, and all went happily enough till I was ten years old. Then one day when I had brought the flock home I never noticed that the Starosta's[12] very best sheep was not among them. And our Starosta was a bad and inhuman peasant. When he came home that evening and found that his sheep was lost, he rushed at me abusing and threatening. If I didn't go off and find the sheep, he swore he'd beat me to death, and 'I'll break your arms and legs,' he said. Knowing how cruel he was, I went after the sheep, searching the places where they had been feeding in daylight. I searched and searched for more than half the night, but there was not a trace of it anywhere. It was such a dark night, too, for it was getting on toward autumn. When I had got very deep into the forest--and in our government the forests are endless--suddenly a storm came up. It was as though the trees were all rocking. In the distance, wolves started howling. Such a terror fell upon me that my hair stood on end. What's more, it all got more and more horrible, so that I was ready to drop with fear and horror. Then I fell on my knees and crossed myself, and

---

[12] *Starosta*. The headman of the village community.

The Pilgrim Continues His Way

with all my heart I said, 'Lord Jesus Christ, have mercy on me.' As soon as I had said that I felt absolutely at peace, straight away, as if I had never been in any distress at all. All my fear left me, and I felt as happy in my heart as if I had flown away to heaven. This made me very glad, and--well, I just didn't stop saying the prayer. To this day I don't know whether the storm lasted long and how the night went. I looked up and daylight was coming, and there was I still kneeling in the same place. I got up quietly, I saw I wouldn't find the sheep, and home I went. But all was well in my heart, and I was saying the prayer to my heart's content. As soon as I got to the village the Starosta saw I hadn't brought the sheep back and thrashed me till I was half dead--he put this foot out of joint, you see. I was laid up, almost unable to move, for six weeks after that beating. All I knew was that I was saying the prayer and it comforted me. When I got a bit better I began to wander about in the world, and as to be continually jostling about in a crowd didn't interest me, and meant a good deal of sin, I took to roaming from one holy place to another, and in the forests too. That's how I have spent nearly five years now."

When I heard this, my heart was very glad that God had thought me fit to meet so good a man, and I asked him, "And do you often use the prayer now?"

"I couldn't exist without it," he answered. "Why, if I only just call to mind how I felt that first time in the forest, it's just as if someone pushed me down on my knees, and I begin to pray. I don't know whether my sinful prayer is pleasing to God or not. For as I pray, sometimes I feel a great happiness--why, I don't know-- a lightness of spirit, a happy sort of quiet; but at other times I feel a dull heaviness and lowness of spirits. But for all that, I want to go on praying always till I die."

"Don't be distressed, dear brother. Everything is pleasing to God and for our salvation--everything, whatever it is that happens in time of prayer. So the Holy Fathers say. Whether it's lightness of heart or heaviness, it's all all right. No prayer, good or bad, fails in God's sight. Lightness, warmth, and gladness show that God is rewarding and consoling us for the effort, while heaviness, darkness, and dryness mean that God is cleansing and strengthening the soul, and by this wholesome trial is saving it, preparing it in humility for the enjoyment of blessed happiness in the future. In proof of this I will read you something that St. John Climacus wrote."

I found the passage and read it to him. He heard it through with care and enjoyed it, and he thanked me very much for it. And so we parted. He went off right into the depth of the forest and I went back to the road. I went on my way, thanking God for treating me, sinner as I am, as fit to be given such teaching.

Next day, by God's help, I came to Kiev. The first and chief thing I wanted was to fast a while and to make my Confession and Communion in that holy town. So I stopped near the Saints[13], as that would be easier for getting to church. A good old Cossack took me in, and as he lived alone in his hut, I found peace and quiet

---

[13] Near the Saints---that is, near where they are buried, the Kiev-Pecherskaya Lavra. This was one of the most famous and influential Monasteries in Russia and was visited by hundreds of thousands of pilgrims every year. It was founded in the eleventh century, and its catacombs still contain the uncorrupted bodies of many saints of ancient Russia.

there. At the end of a week, in which I had been getting ready for my Confession, the thought came to me that I would make it as detailed as I could. So I began to recall and go over my sins from youth onward very fully, and so as not to forget it all I wrote down everything I could remember in the utmost detail. I covered a large sheet of paper with it.

I heard that at Kitaevaya Pustina, about five miles from Kiev, there was a Priest of ascetic life who was very wise and understanding. Whoever went to him for Confession found an atmosphere of tender compassion and came away with teaching for his salvation and ease of spirit. I was very glad to hear of this, and I went to him at once. After I had asked his advise and we had talked awhile, I gave him my sheet of paper to see. He read it through and then said, "Dear friend, a lot of this that you have written is quite futile. Listen: First, don't bring into Confession sins which you have already repented of and had forgiven. Don't go over them again, for that would be to doubt the power of the Sacrament of Confession. Next, don't call to mind other people who have been connected with your sins; judge yourself only. Thirdly, the Holy Fathers forbid us to mention all the circumstances of the sins, and tell us to acknowledge them in general, so as to avoid temptation both for ourselves and for the Priest. Fourthly, you have come to repent and you are not repenting of the fact that you can't repent--that is, your penitence is lukewarm and careless. Fifthly, you have gone over all these details, but the most important thing you have overlooked: you have not disclosed the gravest sins of all. You have not acknowledged, nor written down, that you do not love God, that you hate your neighbor, that you do not believe in God's Word, and that you are filled with pride and ambition. A whole mass of evil, and all our spiritual depravity is in these four sins. They are the chief roots out of which spring the shoots of all the sins into which we fall."

I was very much surprised to hear this, and I said, "Forgive me, Reverend Father, but how is it possible not to love God our Creator and Preserver? What is there to believe in if not the Word of God, in which everything is true and holy? I wish well to all my neighbors, and why should I hate them? I have nothing to be proud of; besides having numberless sins, I have nothing at all which is fit to be praised, and what should I with my poverty and ill-health lust after? Of course, if I were an educated man, or rich, then no doubt I should be guilty of the things you spoke of."

"It's a pity, dear one, that you so little understood what I said. Look! It will teach you more quickly if I give you these notes. They are what I always use for my own Confession. Read them through, and you will see clearly enough an exact proof of what I said to you just now."

He gave me the notes, and I began to read them, as follows:

A CONFESSION WHICH LEADS THE INWARD MAN TO HUMILITY

Turning my eyes carefully upon myself and watching the course of my inward state, I have verified by experience that I do not love God, that I have no love for my neighbors, that I have no religious belief, and that I am filled with pride and sensuality. All this I actually find in myself as a result of detailed examination of my feelings and conduct, thus:

1. I do not love God. For if I loved God I should be continually thinking about Him with heartfelt joy. Every thought of God would give me gladness and delight. On the contrary, I much more often and much more eagerly think about earthly things, and thinking about God is labor and dryness. If I loved God, then talking with Him in prayer would be my nourishment and delight and would draw me to unbroken communion with Him. But, on the contrary, I not only find no delight in prayer, but even find it an effort. I struggle with reluctance, I am enfeebled by sloth and am ready to occupy myself eagerly with any unimportant trifle, if only it shortens prayer and keeps me from it. My time slips away unnoticed in futile occupations, but when I am occupied with God, when I put myself into His presence, every hour seems like a year. If one person loves another, he thinks of him throughout the day without ceasing, he pictures him to himself, he cares for him, and in all circumstances his beloved friend is never out of his thoughts. But I, throughout the day, scarcely set aside even a single hour in which to sink deep down into meditation upon God, to inflame my heart with love of Him, while I eagerly give up twenty-three hours as fervent offerings to the idols of my passions. I am forward in talk about frivolous matters and things which degrade the spirit; that gives me pleasure. But in the consideration of God I am dry, bored, and lazy. Even if I am unwillingly drawn by others into spiritual conversation, I try to shift the subject quickly to one which pleases my desires. I am tirelessly curious about novelties, about civic affairs and political

events; I eagerly seek the satisfaction of my love of knowledge in science and art, and in ways of getting things I want to possess. But the study of the law of God, the knowledge of God and of religion, make little impression on me, and satisfy no hunger of my soul. I regard these things not only as a nonessential occupation for a Christian, but in a casual way as a sort of side-issue with which I should perhaps occupy my spare time, at odd moments. To put it shortly, if love for God is recognized by the keeping of His commandments ("If ye love Me, keep My commandments," says our Lord Jesus Christ), and I not only do not keep them, but even make little attempt to do so, then in absolute truth the conclusion follows that I do not love God. That is what Basil the Great says: "The proof that a man does not love God and His Christ lies in the fact that he does not keep His commandments."

2. I do not love my neighbor either. For not only am I unable to make up my mind to lay down my life for his sake (according to the Gospel), but I do not even sacrifice my happiness, well-being, and peace for the good of my neighbor. If I did love him as myself, as the Gospel bids, his misfortunes would distress me also, his happiness would bring delight to me too. But, on the contrary, I listen to curious, unhappy stories about my neighbor, and I am not distressed; I remain quite undisturbed or, what is still worse, I find a sort of pleasure in them. Bad conduct on the part of my brother I do not cover up with love, but proclaim abroad with censure. His well-being, honor, and happiness do not delight me as my own, and, as if they were something quite alien to me, give me no

feeling of gladness. What is more, they subtly arouse in me feelings of envy or contempt.

3. I have no religious belief. Neither in immortality nor in the Gospel. If I were firmly persuaded and believed without doubt that beyond the grave lies eternal life and recompense for the deeds of this life, I should be continually thinking of this. The very idea of immortality would terrify me and I should lead this life as a foreigner who gets ready to enter his native land. On the contrary, I do not even think about eternity, and I regard the end of this earthly life as the limit of my existence. The secret thought nestles within me: Who knows what happens at death? If I say I believe in immortality, then I am speaking about my mind only, and my heart is far removed from a firm conviction about it. That is openly witnessed to by my conduct and my constant care to satisfy the life of the senses. Were the Holy Gospel taken into my heart in faith, as the Word of God, I should be continually occupied with it, I should study it, find delight in it, and with deep devotion fix my attention upon it. Wisdom, mercy, and love are hidden in it; it would lead me to happiness, I should find gladness in the study of the law of God day and night. In it I should find nourishment like my daily bread, and my heart would be drawn to the keeping of its laws. Nothing on earth would be strong enough to turn me away from it. On the contrary, if now and again I read or hear the Word of God, yet even so it is only from necessity or from a general love of knowledge, and approaching it without any very close attention I find it dull and uninteresting. I usually come to the end of the reading without any profit, only too ready to change

over to secular reading in which I take more pleasure and find new and interesting subjects.

4. I am full of pride and sensual self-love. All my actions confirm this. Seeing something good in myself, I want to bring it into view, or to pride myself upon it before other people or inwardly to admire myself for it. Although I display an outward humility, yet I ascribe it all to my own strength and regard myself as superior to others, or at least no worse than they. If I notice a fault in myself, I try to excuse it; I cover it up by saying, "I am made like that" or "I am not to blame." I get angry with those who do not treat me with respect and consider them unable to appreciate the value of people. I brag about my gifts: my failures in any undertaking I regard as a personal insult. I murmur, and I find pleasure in the unhappiness of my enemies. If I strive after anything good it is for the purpose of winning praise, or spiritual self-indulgence, or earthly consolation. In a word, I continually make an idol of myself and render it uninterrupted service, seeking in all things the pleasures of the senses and nourishment for my sensual passions and lusts.

Going over all this I see myself as proud, adulterous, unbelieving, without love for God and hating my neighbor. What state could be more sinful? The condition of the spirits of darkness is better than mine. They, although they do not love God, hate men, and live upon pride, yet at least believe and tremble. But I? Can there be a doom more terrible than that which faces me, and what sentence of punishment will be more severe than that upon the careless and foolish life that I recognize in myself?

The Pilgrim Continues His Way

On reading through this form of Confession which the Priest gave me I was horrified, and I thought to myself, "Good heavens! What frightful sins there are hidden within me, and up to now I've never noticed them!" The desire to be cleansed from them made me beg this great spiritual father to teach me how to know the causes of all these evils and how to cure them. And he began to instruct me.

"You see, dear brother, the cause of not loving God is want of belief, want of belief is caused by lack of conviction, and the cause of that is failure to seek for holy and true knowledge, indifference to the light of the spirit. In a word, if you don't believe, you can't love; if you are not convinced, you can't believe, and in order to reach conviction you must get a full and exact knowledge of the matter before you. By meditation, by the study of God's Word, and by noting your experience, you must arouse in your soul a thirst and a longing--or, as some call it, 'wonder'-- which brings you an insatiable desire to know things more closely and more fully, to go deeper into their nature.

"One spiritual writer speaks of it in this way: 'Love,' he says, 'usually grows with knowledge, and the greater the depth and extent of the knowledge the more love there will be, the more easily the heart will soften and lay itself open to the love of God, as it diligently gazes upon the very fullness and beauty of the divine nature and His unbounded love for men.'

"So now you see that the cause of those sins which you read over is slothfulness in thinking about spiritual things, sloth which stifles the feeling of the need of such thought. If you want to know how to overcome this evil, strive after enlightenment of spirit by every means in

The Pilgrim Continues His Way

your power, attain it by diligent study of the Word of God and of the Holy Fathers, by the help of meditation and spiritual counsel, and by the conversation of those who are wise in Christ. Ah, dear brother, how much disaster we meet with just because we are lazy about seeking light for our souls through the word of truth. We do not study God's law day and night, and we do not pray about it diligently and unceasingly. And because of this our inner man is hungry and cold, starved, so that it has no strength to take a bold step forward upon the road of righteousness and salvation! And so, beloved, let us resolve to make use of these methods, and as often as possible fill our minds with thoughts of heavenly things; and love, poured down into our hearts from on high, will burst into flame within us. We will do this together and pray as often as we can, for prayer is the chief and strongest means for our renewal and well-being. We will pray, in the words Holy Church teaches us: 'O God, make me fit to love Thee now, as I have loved sin in the past.'[14]"

I listened to all this with care. Deeply moved, I asked this Holy Father to hear my Confession and to give me Communion. And so next morning after the honor of my Communion, I was for going back to Kiev with this blessed viaticum. But this good father of mine, who was going to the Lavra[15] for a couple of days, kept me for that time in his hermit's cell, so that in its silence I might give myself up to prayer without hindrance. And, in fact, I did spend both those days as though I were in

---

[14] From the eighth prayer in the Morning Prayers of the prayer book of the Russian Orthodox Church.

[15] Lavra. Originally a Monastery which followed the rule of St. Anthony, but later used simply to designate certain large Monasteries. Besides Kiev, there were eight Monasteries in Russia that bore the title "Lavra."

heaven. By the prayers of my Starets I, unworthy as I am, rejoiced in perfect peace. Prayer flowed out in my heart so easily and happily that during that time I think I forgot everything, and myself; in my mind was Jesus Christ and He alone.

In the end, the Priest came back, and I asked his guidance and advice--where should I go now on my pilgrim way? He gave me his blessing with these words, "You go to Pochaev, make your reverence there to the wonder-working footprint of the Most Pure Mother of God, and she will guide your feet into the way of peace." And so, taking his advice in faith, three days later I set off for Pochaev.

For some 130 miles or so I traveled none too happily, for the road lay through pot-houses and Jewish villages and I seldom came across a Christian dwelling. At one farm I noticed a Russian Christian inn and I was glad to see it. I turned in at it to spend the night and also to ask for some bread for my journey, for my rusks were coming to an end. Here I saw the host, an old man with a well-to-do air and who, I learned, came from the same government that I did--the Orlovsky. Directly I went into the room, his first question was, "What religion are you?"

I replied that I was a Christian, and Pravoslavny[16]. "Pravoslavny, indeed," said he with a laugh. "You people are Pravoslavny only in word--in act you are heathen. I know all about your religion, brother. A learned Priest once tempted me and I tried it. I joined your church and stayed in it for six months. After that I came back to the ways of our society. To join your

---

[16] *Pravoslavny*. The Russian word for Orthodox. Literally it means "right praising."

147

The Pilgrim Continues His Way

Church is just a snare. The readers mumble the Service all anyhow, with things missed out and things you can't understand. And the singing is no better than you hear in a pub. And the people stand all in a huddle, men and women all mixed up; they talk while the Service is going on, turn round and stare about, walk to and fro, and give you no peace and quiet to say your prayers. What sort of worship do you call that? It's just a sin! Now, with us how devout the Service is; you can hear what's said, nothing is left out, the singing is most moving, and the people stand quietly, the men by themselves, the women by themselves, and everybody knows what reverence to make and when, as Holy Church directs. Really and truly, when you come into a church of ours, you feel you have come to the worship of God; but in one of yours you can't imagine what you've come to--to church or to market!"

From all this I saw that the old man was a diehard raskolnik[17]. But he spoke so plausibly, I could not argue with him nor convert him. I just thought to myself that it

---

[17] *Raskolniki.* Literally "schismatics," sometimes called "Old Believers." In the seventeenth century Nikon, the Patriarch of Moscow, in the face of fierce opposition, carried through a reform of the service books. The Old Believers, led by Avvakum, seceded from the Church rather than accept the changes. The origin of Russian dissent is, therefore, the exact opposite of the origin of English dissent. The *raskolniki* afterward themselves split into more sects, some having a Priesthood and some being without. Some of these sects degenerated into oddities and indulged in the strangest excesses. But the more sober element among the Old Believers incorporates some of the best of Russian religious spirit and character. Altogether these sects numbered some 2 percent of the Christian population of the Empire at the beginning of the twentieth century. There is an English version of the autobiography of the Archpriest Avvakum.

will be impossible to convert the Old Believers to the true Church until Church Services are put right among us, and until the clergy in particular set an example in this. The raskolnik knows nothing of the inner life; he relies upon externals, and it is about them that we are careless.

So I wanted to get away from here and had already gone out into the hall when to my surprise I saw through the open door of a private room a man who did not look like a Russian; he was lying on a bed and reading a book. He beckoned me and asked me who I was. I told him. And then he began, "Listen, dear friend. Won't you agree to look after a sick man, say for a week, until by God's help I get better? I am a Greek, a Monk from Mount Athos. I'm in Russia to collect alms for my Monastery, and on my way back I've fallen ill, so that I can't walk for the pain in my legs. So I've taken this room here. Don't say no, servant of God! I'll pay you."

"There is no need whatever to pay me. I will very gladly look after you as best as I can in the Name of God." So I stayed with him. I heard a great deal from him about the things that concern the salvation of our souls. He told me about Athos, the Holy Mountain, about the great *podvizhniki*[18] there, and about the many hermits and anchorites. He had with him a copy of the *Philokalia* in Greek, and a book by St. Isaac the Syrian. We read together and compared the Slavonic translation by St. Paísy Velichkovsky with the Greek original. He declared that it would be impossible to translate from

---

[18] *Podvizhnik*. A *podvig* is a notable exploit, and the man who performs it is a *podvizhnik*. The terms are applied in the spiritual life to outstanding achievements in the life of prayer and ascetic practices, and to those who attain to them.

Greek more accurately and faithfully than the *Philokalia* had been turned into Slavonic by St. Paísy.

As I noticed that he was always in prayer and versed in the inward Prayer of the Heart, and as he spoke Russian perfectly, I questioned him on this matter. He readily told me a great deal about it, and I listened with care. I even wrote down many things that he said. Thus, for example, he taught me about the excellence and greatness of the Jesus Prayer in this way: "Even the very form of the Jesus Prayer," he said, "shows what a great prayer it is. It is made up of two parts. In the first part, 'Lord Jesus Christ, Son of God,' it leads our thoughts to the life of Jesus Christ, or, as the Holy Fathers put it, it is the whole Gospel in brief. In the second part, 'Have mercy on me, a sinner,' it faces us with the story of our own helplessness and sinfulness. And it is to be noted that the desire and petition of a poor, sinful, humble soul could not be put into words more wise, more clear-cut, more exact than these--'have mercy on me.' No other form of words would be as satisfying and full as this. For instance, if one said, 'Forgive me, put away my sins, cleanse my transgressions, blot out my offenses,' all that would express one petition only--asking to be set free from punishment, the fear of a fainthearted and listless soul. But to say 'have mercy on me' means not only the desire for pardon arising from fear, but is the sincere cry of filial love, which puts its hope in the mercy of God and humbly acknowledges it too weak to break its own will and to keep a watchful guard over itself. It is a cry for mercy--that is, for grace--which will show itself in the gift of strength from God, to enable us to resist temptation and overcome our sinful inclinations. It is like a penniless debtor asking his kindly creditor not only to forgive him the debt but also to pity his extreme poverty and to give him alms--that is

150

what these profound words 'have mercy on me' express. It is like saying, 'Gracious Lord, forgive me my sins and help me to put myself right; arouse in my soul a strong impulse to follow Thy bidding. Bestow Thy grace in forgiving my actual sins and in turning my heedless mind, will, and heart to Thee alone.'"

Upon this I wondered at the wisdom of his words and thanked him for teaching my sinful soul, and he went on teaching me other wonderful things.

"If you like," said he (and I took him to be something of a scholar, for he said he had studied at the Athens Academy), "I will go on and tell you about the tone in which the Jesus Prayer is said. I happen to have heard many God-fearing Christian people say the oral Jesus Prayer as the Word of God bids them and according to the tradition of Holy Church. They use it so both in their private prayers and in church. If you listen carefully and as a friend to this quiet saying of the Prayer, you can notice for your spiritual profit that the tone of the praying voice varies with different people. Thus, some stress the very first word of the prayer and say Lord Jesus Christ, and then finish all the other words on one level tone. Others begin the prayer in a level voice and throw the stress in the middle of the prayer, on the word Jesus as an exclamation, and the rest, again, they finish in an unstressed tone, as they began. Others, again, begin and go on with the prayer without stress until they come to the last words--Have mercy on me--when they raise their voices in ecstasy. And some say the whole prayer--Lord Jesus Christ, Son of God, have mercy on me a sinner--with all the stress upon the single phrase Son of God.

The Pilgrim Continues His Way

"Now listen. The prayer is one and the same. Orthodox Christians hold one and the same profession of faith. The knowledge is common to all of them that this sublime prayer of all prayers includes two things: the Lord Jesus and the appeal to Him. That is known to be the same for everybody. Why then do they not all express it in the same way, why not all in the same tone, that is? Why does the soul plead specially, and express itself with particular stress, not in one and the same place for all, but in a certain place for each? Many say of this that perhaps it is the result of habit, or of copying other people, or that it depends upon a way of understanding the words which corresponds with the individual point of view, or finally that it is just as it comes most easily and naturally to each person. But I think quite differently about it. I should like to look for something higher in it, something unknown not only to the listener, but even to the person who is praying also. May there not be here a hidden moving of the Holy Spirit making intercession for us with groanings which cannot be uttered in those who do not know how and about what to pray? And if everyone prays in the Name of Jesus Christ, by the Holy Spirit, as the Apostle said, the Holy Spirit, who works in secret and gives a prayer to him who prays, may also bestow His beneficent gift upon all, notwithstanding their lack of strength. To one He may give the reverent fear of God, to another love, to another firmness of faith, and to another gracious humility, and so on.

"If this be so, then he who has been given the gift of revering and praising the power of the Almighty will in his prayers stress with special feeling the word Lord, in which he feels the greatness and the might of the Creator of the world. He who has been given the secret outpouring of love in his heart is thrown into rapture and filled with gladness as he exclaims Jesus Christ, just as a certain Starets could not hear the Name of Jesus without a peculiar flood of love and gladness, even in ordinary conversation. The unshakable believer in the Godhead of Jesus Christ, of one substance with the Father, is enkindled with still more fervent faith as he says the words Son of God. One who has received the gift of humility and is deeply aware of his own weakness, with the words have mercy on me is penitent and humbled, and pours out his heart most richly in these last words of the Jesus Prayer. He cherishes hope in the loving kindness of God and abhors his own falling into sin. There you have the causes, in my opinion, of the differing tones in which people say the prayer in the Name of Jesus. And from this you may note as you listen, to the glory of God and your own instruction, by what emotion anyone is specially moved, what spiritual gift any one person has. A number of people have said to me on this subject, 'Why do not all these signs of hidden spiritual gifts appear together and united? Then not only one, but every word of the prayer would be imbued with one and the same tone of rapture.' I have answered in this way: 'Since the Grace of God distributes His gift in wisdom to every man severally according to his strength, as we see from Holy Scripture, who can search out with his finite mind and enter into the dispositions of grace? Is not the clay completely in the power of the potter, and is he not able to make one thing or another out of the clay?'"

I spent five days with this Starets, and he began to get very much better in health. This time was of so much profit to me that I did not notice how quickly it went. For in that little room, in silent seclusion, we were concerned with nothing else whatever than silent prayer in the Name of Jesus, or talk about the same subject, interior prayer.

One day a pilgrim came to see us. He complained bitterly about the Jews and abused them. He had been going about their villages and had to put up with their unfriendliness and cheating. He was so bitter against them that he cursed them, even saying they were not fit to live because of their obstinacy and unbelief. Finally he said that he had such an aversion for them that it was quite beyond his control.

"You have no right, friend," said the Starets, "to abuse and curse the Jews like this. God made them just as He made us. You should be sorry for them and pray for them, not curse them. Believe me, the disgust you feel for them comes from the fact that you are not grounded in the love of God and have no interior prayer as a security and, therefore, no inward peace. I will read you a passage from the Holy Fathers about this. Listen, this is what St. Mark the Ascetic writes: 'The soul which is inwardly united to God becomes, in the greatness of its joy, like a good-natured, simple-hearted child, and now condemns no one, Greek, heathen, Jew, nor sinner, but looks at them all alike with sight that has been cleansed, finds joy in the whole world, and wants everybody--Greeks and Jews and heathen--to praise God.' And St. Macarius the Great, of Egypt, says that the inward contemplative 'burns with so great a love that if it were possible he would have everyone dwell within him, making no difference between bad and good.' There, dear brother, you see what the Holy Fathers think about it. So I advise you to lay aside your fierceness, and look upon everything as under the all-knowing providence of God, and when you meet with vexations accuse yourself especially of lack of patience and humility."

At last more than a week went by and my Starets got well, and I thanked him from my heart for all the blessed instruction that he had given me, and we said good-bye. He set off for home and I started upon the way I had planned. Now I began to get near to Pochaev. I had not gone more than seventy miles when a soldier overtook me, and I asked him where he was going. He told me he was going back to his native district in Kamenets Podolsk. We went along in silence for seven miles or so, and I noticed that he sighed very heavily as though something were distressing him, and he was very gloomy. I asked him why he was so sad.

"Good friend, if you have noticed my sorrow and will swear by all you hold sacred never to tell anybody, I will tell you all about myself, for I am near to death and I have no one to talk to about it."

I assured him, as a Christian, that I had not the slightest need to tell anybody about it, and that out of brotherly love I should be glad to give him any advice that I could.

"Well, you see," he began, "I was drafted as a soldier from the state peasants. After about five years' service it became intolerably hard for me; in fact, they often flogged me for negligence and for drunkenness. I took it into my head to run away, and here I am a deserter for the last fifteen years. For six years I hid wherever I could. I stole from farms and larders and warehouses. I stole horses. I broke into shops and followed this sort of trade, always on my own. I got rid of my stolen goods in various ways. I drank the money, I led a depraved life,

155

committed every sin. Only my soul didn't perish. I got on very well, but in the end I got into jail for wandering without a passport. But when a chance came I even escaped from there. Then unexpectedly I met with a soldier who had been discharged from the service and was going home to a distant government. As he was ill and could hardly walk he asked me to take him to the nearest village where he could find lodging. So I took him. The police allowed us to spend the night in a barn on some hay, and there we lay down. When I woke up in the morning I glanced at my soldier and there he was dead and stiff. Well, I hurriedly searched for his passport--that is to say, his discharge--and when I found it and a fair amount of money too, while everybody was still asleep, I was out of the shed and the backyard as quickly as I could, and so into the forest, and off I went. On reading his passport I saw that in age and distinguishing marks he was almost the same as I. I was very glad about this and went on boldly into the depths of the Astrakhan government. There I began to steady down a bit and I got a job as a laborer. I joined up with an old man there who had his own house and was a cattle dealer. He lived alone with his daughter, who was a widow. When I had lived with him for a year, I married this daughter of his. Then the old man died. We could not carry on the business. I started drinking again, and my wife too, and in a year we had gone though everything the old man had left. And then my wife took ill and died. So I sold everything that was left, and the house, and I soon ran through the money.

"Now I had nothing to live on, nothing to eat. So I went back to my old trade of dealing in stolen goods, and all the more boldly now because I had a passport. So I took to my old evil life again for about a year. There came a time when for a long while I met with no success. I stole an old wretched horse from a bobil[19] and I sold it to the knacker for a small sum. Taking the money, I went off to a pub and began to drink. I had an idea of going to a village where there was a wedding, and while everybody was asleep after the feasting I meant to pick up whatever I could. As the sun had not yet set I went into the forest to wait for night. I lay down there and fell into a deep sleep. Then I had a dream and saw myself standing in a wide and beautiful meadow. Suddenly a terrible cloud began to rise in the sky, and then there came such a terrific clap of thunder that the ground trembled underneath me, and it was as though someone drove me up to my shoulders into the ground, which jammed against me on all sides. Only my head and my hands were left outside. Then this terrible cloud seemed to come down onto the ground and out of it came my grandfather, who had been dead for twenty years. He was a very upright man and for thirty years was a church warden in our village. With an angry and threatening face he came up to me and I shook with fear. Round about nearby I saw several heaps of things which I had stolen at various times. I was still more frightened. My grandfather came up to me and, pointing to the first heap, said threateningly, 'What is that? Let him have it!' And suddenly the ground on all sides of me began to squeeze me so hard that I could not bear the pain and the faintness. I groaned and cried out, 'Have mercy on me,' but the torment went on. Then my grandfather pointed to another heap and said again, 'What is that? Crush him harder!' And I felt such violent pain and agony that no torture on earth could compare with it. Finally, that grandfather of mine brought near me the horse that I had stolen the evening before, and cried out, 'And what is this? Let him have it as hard as

---

[19] *Bobil.* A landless peasant, hence a miserable, poverty-stricken fellow.

you can.' And I got such pain from all sides that I can't describe it, it was so cruel, terrible, and exhausting. It was as though all my sinews were being drawn out of me and I was suffocated by the frightful pain. I felt I could not bear it and that I should collapse unconscious if that torture went on even a little bit longer. But the horse kicked out and caught me on the cheek and cut it open, and the moment I got that blow I woke up in utter horror and shaking like a weakling. I saw that it was already daylight, the sun was rising. I touched my cheek and blood was flowing from it; and those parts of me which in my dream had been in the ground were all hard and stiff and I had pins and needles in them. I was in such terror that I would hardly get up and go home. My cheek hurt for a long time. Look, you can see the scar now. It wasn't there before. And so, after this, fear and horror often used to come over me and now I only have to remember what I suffered in that dream for the agony and exhaustion to begin again and such torture that I don't know what to do with myself. What is more, it began to come more often, and in the end I began to be afraid of people and to feel ashamed as though everybody knew my past dishonesty. Then I could neither eat nor drink nor sleep because of this suffering. I was worn to a ravel. I did think of going to my regiment and making a clean breast of everything. Perhaps God would forgive my sins if I took my punishment. But I was afraid, and I lost my courage because they would make me run the gauntlet. And so, losing patience, I wanted to hang myself. But the thought came to me that in any case I shan't live for a very long time; I shall soon die, for I have lost all my strength. And so I thought I would go and say good-bye to my home and die there. I have a nephew at home. And here I am on my way there for six months now. And all the while grief and fear make me miserable.

The Pilgrim Continues His Way

What do you think, my friend? What am I to do? I really can't bear much more."

When I heard all this I was astonished, and I praised the wisdom and the goodness of God, as I saw the different ways in which they are brought to sinners. So I said to him, "Dear brother, during the time of that fear and agony you ought to have prayed to God. That is the great cure for all our troubles."

"Not on your life!" he said to me. "I thought that as soon as I began to pray, God would destroy me."

"Nonsense, brother; it is the devil who puts thoughts like that into your head. There is no end to God's mercy and He is sorry for sinners and quickly forgives all who repent. Perhaps you don't know the Jesus Prayer: 'Lord Jesus Christ, have mercy on me, a sinner.' You go on saying that without stopping."

"Why, of course I know that Prayer. I used to say it sometimes to keep my courage up when I was going to do a robbery."

"Now, look here. God did not destroy you when you were on your way to do something wrong and said the Prayer. Will He do so when you start praying on the path of repentance? Now, you see how your thoughts come from the devil. Believe me, dear brother, if you will say that Prayer, taking no notice of whatever thoughts come into your mind, then you will quickly feel relief. All the fear and strain will go, and in the end you will be completely at peace. You will become a devout man, and all sinful passions will leave you. I assure you of this, for I have seen a great deal of it in my time."

After that I told him about several cases in which the Jesus Prayer had shown its wonderful power to work upon sinners. In the end I persuaded him to come with me to the Pochaev Mother of God, the Refuge of Sinners, before he went home, and to make his Confession and Communion there.

My soldier listened to all this attentively and, as I could see, with joy, and he agreed to everything. We went to Pochaev together on this condition, that neither of us should speak to the other, but that we should say the Jesus Prayer all the time. In this silence we walked for a whole day. Next day he told me that he felt much easier, and it was plain that his mind was calmer than before. On the third day we arrived at Pochaev, and I urged him again not to break off the Prayer either day or night while he was awake, and assured him that the most Holy Name of Jesus, which is unbearable to our spiritual foes, would be strong to save him. On this point I read to him from the *Philokalia* that although we ought to say the Jesus Prayer at all times, it is especially needful to do so with the utmost care when we are preparing for Communion.

So he did, and then he made his Confession and Communion. Although from time to time the old thoughts still came over him, yet he easily drove them away with the Jesus Prayer. On Sunday, so as to be up for Matins more easily, he went to bed earlier and went on saying the Jesus Prayer. I still sat in the corner and read my *Philokalia* by a rushlight. An hour went past; he fell asleep and I set myself to prayer. All of a sudden, about twenty minutes later, he gave a start and woke up, jumped quickly out of bed, ran over to me in tears, and, speaking with the greatest happiness, he said, "Oh brother, what I have just seen! How peaceful and happy I am; I believe that God has mercy upon sinners and does not torment them. Glory to Thee, O Lord, glory to Thee."

I was surprised and glad and asked him to tell me exactly what had happened to him.

"Why, this," he said. "As soon as I fell asleep I saw myself in that meadow where they tortured me. At first I was terrified, but I saw that, instead of a cloud, the bright sun was rising and a wonderful light was shining over the whole meadow. And I saw red flowers and grass in it. Then suddenly my grandfather came up to me, looking nicer than you ever saw, and he greeted me gently and kindly. And he said, 'Go to Zhitomir, to the Church of St. George. They will take you under Church protection. Spend the rest of your life there and pray without ceasing. God will be gracious to you.' When he said this he made the Sign of the Cross over me and straight away vanished. I can't tell you how happy I felt; it was as though a load had been taken off my shoulders and I had flown away to heaven. At that point I woke up, feeling easy in my mind and my heart so full of joy that I didn't know what to do. What ought I to do now? I shall start straight away for Zhitomir, as my grandfather told me. I shall find it easy going with the prayer."

"But wait a minute, dear brother. How can you start off in the middle of the night? Stay for Matins, say your prayers, and then start off with God."

So we didn't go to sleep after this conversation. We went to church; he stayed all through Matins, praying earnestly with tears, and he said that he felt very peaceful and glad and that the Jesus Prayer was going on happily. Then after the Liturgy he made his Communion, and when we had had some food I went with him as far as the Zhitomir road, where we said good-bye with tears of gladness.

After this I began to think about my own affairs. Where should I go now? In the end I decided that I would go back again to Kiev. The wise teaching of my Priest there drew me that way, and besides, if I stayed with him he might find some Christ-loving philanthropist who would put me on my way to Jerusalem or at least to Mount Athos. So I stopped another week at Pochaev, spending the time in recalling all I had learned from those I had met on this journey and in making notes of a number of helpful things. Then I got ready for the journey, put on my kotomka, and went to church to commend my journey to the Mother of God. When the Liturgy was over I said my prayers and was ready to start. I was standing at the back of the church when a man came in, not very richly dressed, but clearly one of the gentry, and he asked me where the candles were sold. I showed him. At the end of the Liturgy I stayed praying at the shrine of the footprint. When I had finished my prayers I set off on my way. I had gone a little way along the street when I saw an open window in one of the houses at which a man sat reading a book. My way took me past that very window and I saw that the man sitting there was the same one who had asked me about the candles in church. As I went by I took off my hat, and when he saw me he beckoned me to come to him, and said, "I suppose you must be a pilgrim?"

The Pilgrim Continues His Way

"Yes," I answered.

He asked me in and wanted to know who I was and where I was going. I told him all about myself and hid nothing. He gave me some tea and began to talk to me.

"Listen, my little pigeon, I should advise you to go to the Solovetsky[20] Monastery. There is a very secluded and peaceful Skete[21] there called Anzersky. It is like a second Athos and they welcome everybody there. The novitiate consists only in this: that they take turns to read the Psalter in church four hours out of the twenty-four. I am going there myself and I have taken a vow to go on foot. We might go together. I should be safer with you; they say it is a very lonely road. On the other hand, I have got money and I could supply you with food the whole way. And I should propose we went on these terms, that we walked half a dozen yards apart; then we should not be in each other's way, and as we went we could spend the time in reading all the while or in meditation. Think it over, brother, and do agree; it will be worth your while."

When I heard this invitation I took this unexpected event as a sign for my journey from the Mother of God whom I had asked to teach me the way to blessedness. And without further thought I agreed at once. And so we set out the next day. We walked for three days, as we had agreed, one behind the other. He read a book the whole time, a book which never left his hand day or night; and at times he was meditating about something.

---

[20] Solovetsky. The famous Monastery on the group of islands of that name in the White Sea. It was founded in 1429 by St. German and St. Sabbas. The former had been a Monk of Valaam.

[21] Skete. A small monastic community dependent upon a large Monastery.

The Pilgrim Continues His Way

At last we came to a halt at a certain place for dinner. He ate his food with the book lying open in front of him and he was continually looking at it. I saw that the book was a copy of the Gospels, and I said to him, "May I venture to ask, sir, why you never allowed the Gospels out of your hand day or night? Why you always hold it and carry it with you?"

"Because," he answered, "from it and it alone I am almost continually learning."

"And what are you learning?" I went on.

"The Christian life, which is summed up in prayer. I consider that prayer is the most important and necessary means of salvation and the first duty of every Christian. Prayer is the first step in the devout life and also its crown, and that is why the Gospel bids unceasing prayer. To other acts of piety their own times are assigned, but in the matter of prayer there are no off times. Without prayer it is impossible to do any good and without the Gospel you cannot learn properly about prayer. Therefore, all those who have reached salvation by way of the interior life, the holy preachers of the Word of God, as well as hermits and recluses, and indeed all God-fearing Christians, were taught by their unfailing and constant occupation with the depths of God's Word and by reading the Gospel. Many of them had the Gospel constantly in their hands, and in their teaching about salvation gave the advise, 'Sit down in the silence of your cell and read the Gospel and read it again.' There you have the reason why I concern myself with the Gospel alone."

I was very much pleased with this reasoning of his and with his eagerness for prayer. I went on to ask him from which Gospel in particular he got the teaching about prayer. "From all four Evangelists," he answered; "in a word, from the whole of the New Testament, reading it in order. I have been reading it for a long time and taking in the meaning, and it has shown me that there is a graduation and a regular chain of teaching about prayer in the holy Gospels, beginning from the first Evangelist and going right through in a regular order, in a system. For instance, at the very beginning there is laid down the approach, or the introduction to teaching about prayer; then the form or the outward expression of it in words. Farther on we have the necessary conditions upon which prayer may be offered, the means of learning it, and examples; and finally the secret teaching about interior and spiritual ceaseless prayer in the Name of Jesus Christ, which is set forth as higher and more salutary than formal prayer. And then comes its necessity, its blessed fruit, and so on. In a word, there it to be found in the Gospel full and detailed knowledge about the practice of prayer, in systematic order or sequence from beginning to end."

When I heard this I decided to ask him to show me all this in detail. So I said, "As I like hearing and talking about prayer more than anything else, I should be very glad indeed to see this secret chain of teaching about prayer in all its details. For the love of God, then, show me all this in the Gospel itself."

He readily agreed to this and said, "Open your Gospel; look at it and make notes about what I say." And he gave me a pencil. "Be so good as to look at these notes of mine. Now," said he, "look first of all in the Gospel of St. Matthew the sixth chapter, and read from the fifth to the ninth verses. You see that here we have the preparation or the introduction, teaching that not for vainglory and noisily, but in a solitary place and in quietude we should begin our prayer, and pray only for forgiveness of sins and for communion with God, and not devising many and unnecessary petitions about various worldly things as the heathen do. Then, read farther on in the same chapter, from the ninth to the fourteenth verses. Here the form of prayer is given to us--that is to say, in what sort of words it ought to be expressed. There you have brought together in great wisdom everything that is necessary and desirable for our life. After that, go on and read the fourteenth and fifteenth verses of the same chapter, and you will see the conditions it is necessary to observe so that prayer may be effective. For unless we forgive those who have injured us, God will not forgive our sins. Pass on now to the seventh chapter, and you will find in the seventh to the twelfth verses how to succeed in prayer to be bold in hope--ask, seek, knock. These strong expressions depict frequency in prayer and the urgency of practicing it, so that prayer shall not only accompany all actions but even come before them in time. This constitutes the principal property of prayer. You will see an example of this in the fourteenth chapter of St. Mark and the thirty-second to the fortieth verses, where Jesus Christ Himself repeats the same words of prayer frequently. St. Luke, chapter eleven, verses five to fourteen, gives a similar example of repeated prayer in the parable of the friend at midnight and the repeated request of the importunate widow (Luke 18:1-8), illustrating the command of Jesus Christ that we should pray always, at all times and in every place, and not grow discouraged-- that is to say, not get lazy. After this detailed teaching we have shown to us in the Gospel of St. John the essential teaching about the secret interior Prayer of the Heart. In the first place we are shown it in the profound story of the conversation of Jesus Christ with the woman of Samaria, in which is revealed the interior worship of God 'in spirit and in truth' which God desires and which is unceasing true prayer, like living water flowing into eternal life (John 4:5-25). Farther on, in the fifteenth chapter, verses four to eight, there is pictured for us still more decidedly the power and the might and the necessity of inward prayer--that is to say, of the presence of the spirit in Christ in unceasing remembrance of God. Finally, read verses twenty-three to twenty-five in the sixteenth chapter of the same Evangelist. See what a mystery is revealed here. You notice that prayer in the Name of Jesus Christ, or what is known as the Jesus Prayer--that is to say, 'Lord Jesus Christ, have mercy on me'--when frequently repeated, has the greatest power and very easily opens the heart and blesses it. This is to be noticed very clearly in the case of the Apostles, who had been for a whole year disciples of Jesus Christ, and had already been taught the Lord's Prayer by Him--that is to say, 'Our Father' (and it is through them that we know it). Yet at the end of His earthly life Jesus Christ revealed to them the mystery that was still lacking in their prayers. So that their prayer might make a definite step forward He said to them, 'Hitherto have ye asked nothing in My Name. Verily I say unto you, whatsoever ye shall ask the Father in My Name He will give it you.' And so it happened in their case. For, ever after this time, when the Apostles learned to offer prayers in the Name of Jesus Christ, how many wonderful works they performed and what abundant light was shed upon them. Now, do you see the chain, the fullness of teaching about prayer deposited with such wisdom in the Holy Gospel? And if you go on after this to the reading of the Apostolic Epistles, in them also you can find the same successive teaching about prayer.

The Pilgrim Continues His Way

"To continue the notes I have already given you I will show you several places which illustrate the properties of prayer. Thus, in the Acts of the Apostles the practice of it is described--that is to say, the diligent and constant exercise of prayer by the first Christians, who were enlightened by their faith in Jesus Christ (Acts 4:31). The fruits of prayer are told to us, or the results of being constantly in prayer--that is to say, the outpouring of the Holy Spirit and His gifts upon those who pray. You will see something similar to this in the sixteenth chapter, verses twenty-five and twenty-six. Then follow it up in order in the Apostolic Epistles and you will see (1) how necessary prayer is in all circumstance (James 5:13-16); (2) how the Holy Spirit helps us to pray (Jude 20-21 and Rom. 8:26); (3) how we ought all to pray in the Spirit (Eph. 6:18); (4) how necessary calm and inward peace are to prayer (Phil. 4:6, 7); (5) how necessary it is to pray without ceasing (1 Thess. 5:17); (6) and finally we notice that one ought to pray not only for oneself but also for all men (1 Tim. 2:1-5). Thus, by spending a long time with great care in drawing out the meaning we can find many more revelations still of secret knowledge hidden in the Word of God, which escape one if one reads it but rarely or hurriedly.

"Do you notice, after what I have now shown you, with what wisdom and how systematically the New Testament reveals the teaching of our Lord Jesus Christ on this matter, which we have been tracing? In what a wonderful sequence it is put in all four Evangelists? It is like this. In St. Matthew we see the approach, the introduction to prayer, the actual form of prayer, conditions of it, and so on. Go farther. In St. Mark we find examples. In St. Luke, parables. In St. John, the secret exercise of inward prayer, although this is also

168

found in all four Evangelists, either briefly or at length. In the Acts the practice of prayer and the results of prayer are pictured for us; in the Apostolic Epistles, and in the Apocalypse itself, are many properties inseparably connected with the act of prayer. And there you have the reason that I am content with the Gospels alone as my teacher in all the ways of salvation."

All the while he was showing me this and teaching me I marked in the Gospels (in my Bible) all the places which he pointed out to me. It seemed to me most remarkable and instructive, and I thanked him very much.

Then we went on for another five days in silence. My fellow-pilgrim's feet began to hurt him very much, no doubt because he was not used to continuous walking. So he hired a cart with a pair of horses and took me with him. And so we have come into your neighborhood and have stayed here for three days, so that when we have had some rest we can set off straight away to Anzersky, where he is so anxious to go.

The Starets. This friend of yours is splendid. Judging from his piety he must be very well instructed. I should like to see him.

The Pilgrim. We are stopping in the same place. Let me bring him to you tomorrow. It is late now. Goodbye.

Chapter II

The Pilgrim. As I promised when I saw you yesterday, I have asked my revered fellow-pilgrim, who solaced my pilgrim way with spiritual conversation and whom you wanted to see, to come here with me.

The Starets. It will be very nice both for me and, I hope, also for these revered visitors of mine, to see you both and to have the advantage of hearing your experiences. I have with me here a venerable *skhimnik*[22], and here a devout Priest. And so, where two or three are gathered together in the Name of Jesus Christ, there He promises to be present. And now, here are five of us in His Name, and so no doubt He will vouchsafe to bless us all the more bountifully. The story which your fellow-pilgrim told me yesterday, dear brother, about your burning attachment to the Holy Gospel, is most notable and instructive. It would be interesting to know in what way this great and blessed secret was revealed to you.

The Professor. The all-loving God, who desires that all men should be saved and come to the knowledge of the truth, revealed it to me of His great loving-kindness in a marvelous way, without any human intervention. For five years I was a professor and I led a gloomy

---

[22] *Skhimnik* (fem. *Skhimnitsa*). Lit. "habit," as in, possessing the full monastic habit. A Monk (Nun) of the highest grade. The distinction between simple and solemn vows which has arisen in the West has never found a place in Orthodox monasticism. In the latter, Religious are of three grades, distinguished by their habit, and the highest grade is pledged to a stricter degree of asceticism and a greater amount of time spent in prayer. The Russian *skhimnik* is the Greek *Megaloschemos*.

dissipated sort of life, captivated by the vain philosophy of the world, and not according to Christ. Perhaps I should have perished altogether had I not been upheld to some extent by the fact that I lived with my very devout mother and my sister, who was a serious-minded young woman. One day, when I was taking a walk along the public boulevard, I met and made the acquaintance of an excellent young man who told me he was a Frenchman, a student who had not long ago arrived from Paris and was looking for a post as tutor. His high degree of culture delighted me very much, and he being a stranger in this country I asked him to my home and we became friends. In the course of two months he frequently came to see me. Sometimes we went for walks together and amused ourselves and went together into company which I leave you to suppose was very immoral. At length he came to me one day with an invitation to a place of that sort; and in order to persuade me more quickly he began to praise the particular liveliness and pleasantness of the company to which he was inviting me. After he had been speaking about it for a short while, suddenly he began to ask me to come with him out of my study where we were sitting and to sit in the drawing room. This seemed to me very odd. So I said that I had never before noticed any reluctance on his part to be in my study, and what, I asked, was the cause of it now? And I added that the drawing room was next door to the room where my mother and sister were, and for us to carry on this sort of conversation there would be unseemly. He pressed his point on various pretexts, and finally came out quite openly with this: "Among those books on your shelves there you have a copy of the Gospels. I have such a reverence for that book that in its presence I find a difficulty in talking about our disreputable affairs. Please take it away from here; then we can talk freely."

The Pilgrim Continues His Way

In my frivolous way I smiled at his words. Taking the Gospels from the shelf I said, "You ought to have told me that long ago," and handed it to him, saying, "Well, take it yourself and put it down somewhere in the room." No sooner had I touched him with the Gospels than at that instant he trembled and disappeared. This dumbfounded me to such an extent that I fell senseless to the floor with fright. Hearing the noise, my household came running in to me, and for a full half hour they were unable to bring me to my senses. In the end, when I came to myself again, I was frightened and shaky and I felt thoroughly upset, and my hands and my feet were absolutely numb so that I could not move them. When the doctor was called in he diagnosed paralysis as the result of some great shock or fright. I was laid up for a whole year after this, and with the most careful medical attention from many doctors I did not get the smallest alleviation, so that as a result of my illness it looked as though I should have to resign my position. My mother, who was growing old, died during this period, and my sister was preparing to become a Nun, and all this increased my illness all the more. I had but one consolation during this time of sickness, and that was reading the Gospel, which from the beginning of my illness never left my hands. It was a sort of pledge of the marvelous thing that had happened to me. One day an unknown recluse came to see me. He was making a collection for his Monastery. He spoke to me very persuasively and told me that I should not rely only upon medicines, which without the help of God were unable to bring me relief, and that I should pray to God and pray diligently about this very thing, for prayer is the most powerful means of healing all sicknesses both bodily and spiritual.

The Pilgrim Continues His Way

"How can I pray in such a position as this, when I have not the strength to make any sort of reverence, nor can I lift my hands to cross myself?" I answered in my bewilderment. To this he said, "Well, at any rate, pray somehow." But farther he did not go, nor actually explain to me how to pray. When my visitor left me I seemed almost involuntarily to start thinking about prayer and about its power and its effects, calling to mind the instruction I had had in religious knowledge long ago when I was still a student. This occupied me very happily and renewed in my mind my knowledge of religious matters, and it warmed my heart. At the same time I began to feel a certain relief in my attack of illness. Since the book of the Gospels was continually with me, such was my faith in it as the result of the miracle; and as I remembered also that the whole discourse upon prayer which I had heard in lectures was based upon the Gospel text, I considered that the best thing would be to make a study of prayer and Christian devotion solely upon the teaching of the Gospel. Working out its meaning, I drew upon it as from an abundant spring, and found a complete system of the life of salvation and of true interior prayer. I reverently marked all the passages on this subject, and from that time I have been trying zealously to learn this divine teaching, and with all my might, though not without difficulty, to put it into practice. While I was occupied in this way, my health gradually improved, and in the end, as you see, I recovered completely. As I was still living alone I decided in thankfulness to God for His fatherly kindness, which had given me recovery of health and enlightenment of mind, to follow the example of my sister and prompting of my own heart, and to dedicate myself to the solitary life, so that unhindered I might receive and make my own those sweet words of eternal life given me in the Word of

God. So here I am at the present time, stealing off to the solitary Skete in the Solovetsky Monastery in the White Sea, which is called Anzersky, about which I have heard on good authority that it is a most suitable place for the contemplative life. Further, I will tell you this. The Holy Gospel gives me much consolation in this journey of mine, and sheds abundant light upon my untutored mind, and warms my chilly heart. Yet the fact is that in spite of all I frankly acknowledge my weakness, and I freely admit that the conditions of fulfilling the work of devotion and attaining salvation, the requirement of thoroughgoing self-denial, of extraordinary spiritual achievements, and of most profound humility which the Gospel enjoins, frighten me by their very magnitude and in view of the weak and damaged state of my heart. So that I stand now between despair and hope. I don't know what will happen to me in the future.

The Skhimnik. With such an evident token of a special and miraculous mercy of God, and in view of your education, it would be unpardonable not only to give way to depression, but even to admit into your soul a shadow of doubt about God's protection and help. Do you know what the God-enlightened Chrysostom says about this? "No one should be depressed," he teaches, "and give the false impression that the precepts of the Gospel are impossible or impracticable. God who has predestined the salvation of man has, of course, not laid commandments upon him with the intention of making him an offender because of their impracticability. No, but so that by their holiness and the necessity of them for a virtuous life they may be a blessing to us, as in this life so in eternity." Of course the regular unswerving fulfillment of God's commandments is extraordinarily difficult for our fallen nature and, therefore, salvation is not easily attained, but that same Word of God which lays down the commandments offers also the means not only for their ready fulfillment, but also comfort in the fulfilling of them. If this is hidden at first sight behind a veil of mystery, then that, of course, is in order to make us betake ourselves the more to humility, and to bring us more easily into union with God by indicating direct recourse to Him in prayer and petition for His fatherly help. It is there that the secret of salvation lies, and not in reliance upon one's own efforts.

The Pilgrim. How I should like, weak and feeble as I am, to get to know that secret, so that I might to some extent, at least, put my slothful life right, for the glory of God and my own salvation.

The Skhimnik. The secret is known to you, dear brother, from your book the *Philokalia*. It lies in that unceasing prayer of which you have made so resolute a study and in which you have so zealously occupied yourself and found comfort.

The Pilgrim. I fall at your feet, Reverend Father. For the love of God let me hear something for my good from your lips about this saving mystery and about holy prayer, which I long to hear about more than anything else, and about which I love reading to get strength and comfort for my sinful soul.

The Skhimnik. I cannot satisfy your wish with my own thoughts on this exalted subject, because I have had but very little experience of it myself. But I have some very clearly written notes by a spiritual writer precisely on this subject. If the rest of those who are talking with us would like it, I will get it at once and with your permission I can read it to you all.

All. Do be so kind, Reverend Father. Do not keep such saving knowledge from us.

THE SECRET OF SALVATION, REVEALED BY UNCEASING PRAYER

The Skhimnik. How one is saved? This godly question naturally arises in the mind of every Christian who realizes the injured and enfeebled nature of man, and what is left of its original urge toward truth and righteousness. Everyone who has even some degree of faith in immortality and recompense in the life to come is involuntarily faced by the thought, "How am I to be saved?" when he turns his eyes toward heaven. When he tries to find a solution to this problem, he inquires of the wise and learned. Then under their guidance he reads edifying books by spiritual writers on this subject, and sets himself unswervingly to follow out the truths and the rules he has heard and read. In all these instructions he finds constantly put before him as necessary conditions of salvation a devout life and heroic struggles with himself which are to issue in decisive denial of self. This is to lead him on to the performance of good works, to the constant fulfillment of God's laws, and thus witness to the unshakableness and firmness of his faith. Further, they preach to him that all these conditions of salvation must necessarily be fulfilled with the deepest humility and in combination with one another. For as all good works depend on one another, so they should support one another, complete and encourage one another, just as the rays of the sun only reveal their strength and kindle a flame when they are focused through a glass on to one point. Otherwise, "He that is unjust in the least is unjust also in much."

The Pilgrim Continues His Way

In addition to this, to implant in him the strongest conviction of the necessity of this complex and unified virtue, he hears the highest praise bestowed upon the beauty of virtue, he listens to censure of the baseness and misery of vice. All this is imprinted upon his mind by truthful promises either of majestic rewards and happiness or of tormenting punishment and misery in the life to come. Such is the special character of preaching in modern times. Guided in this way, one who ardently wishes for salvation sets off in all joy to carry out what he has learned and to apply to experience all he has heard and read. But alas! even at the first step he finds it impossible to achieve his purpose. He foresees and even finds out by trial that his damaged and enfeebled nature will have the upper hand of the convictions of his mind, that his free will is bound, that his propensities are perverted, that his spiritual strength is but weakness. He naturally goes on to the thought: Is there not to be found some kind of means which will enable him to fulfill that which the law of God requires of him, which Christian devotion demands, and which all those who have found salvation and holiness have carried out? As the result of this and in order to reconcile in himself the demands of reason and conscience with the inadequacy of his strength to fulfill them, he applies once more to the preachers of salvation with the question: How am I to be saved? How is this inability to carry out the conditions of salvation to be justified; and are those who have preached all this that he has learned themselves strong enough to carry it out unswervingly?

Ask God. Pray to God. Pray for His help.

"So would it not have been more fruitful," the inquirer concludes, "if I had, to begin with and always

177

in every circumstance, made a study of prayer as the power to fulfill all that Christian devotion demands and by which salvation is attained?" And so he goes on to the study of prayer: he reads, he meditates, he studies the teaching of those who have written on that subject. Truly he finds in them many luminous thoughts, much deep knowledge, and words of great power. One reasons beautifully about the necessity of prayer; another writes of its power, its beneficial effect--of prayer as a duty, or of the fact that it calls for zeal, attention, warmth of heart, purity of mind, reconciliation with one's enemies, humility, contrition, and the rest of the necessary conditions of prayer. But what is prayer in itself? How does one actually pray? A precise answer which can be understood by everybody to these questions, primary and most urgent as they are, is very rarely to be found, and so the ardent inquirer about prayer is again left before a veil of mystery. As a result of his general reading there is rooted in his memory an aspect of prayer which, although devout, is only external, and he arrives at the conclusion that prayer is going to church, crossing oneself, bowing, kneeling, and reading Psalms, Canons[23], and Akathists. Generally speaking, this is the view of prayer taken by those who do not know the writings of the Holy Fathers about inward prayer and contemplative action. At length, the seeker comes across the book called *Philokalia*, in which twenty-five Holy Fathers set forth in an understandable way the scientific knowledge of the truth and of the essence of Prayer of the Heart. This

---

[23] The Canon could be defined as a liturgical poem following a set pattern, based upon the nine Biblical Canticles which are found throughout the Old and New Testaments. Canons are chanted as a part of the fixed cycle of Divine Services (for instance, at Matins and Compline) and are also chanted privately for devotional purposes –ed.

begins to draw aside the veil from before the secret of salvation and of prayer. He sees that truly to pray means to direct the thought and the memory, without relaxing, to the recollection of God, to walk in His divine presence, to awaken oneself to His love by thinking about Him, and to link the Name of God with one's breathing and the beating of one's heart. He is guided in all this by the invocation with the lips of the most Holy Name of Jesus Christ, or by saying the Jesus Prayer at all times and in all places and during every occupation, unceasingly. These luminous truths, by enlightening the mind of the seeker and by opening up before him the way to the study and achievement of prayer, help him to go on at once to put these wise teachings into practice. Nevertheless, when he makes his attempts he is still not free from difficulty until an experienced teacher shows him (from the same book) the whole truth--that is to say, that it is prayer which is unceasing which is the only effective means for perfecting interior prayer and for saving of the soul. It is frequency of prayer that is the basis, that holds together the whole system of saving activity. As Simeon the New Theologian says, "He who prays without ceasing unites all good in this one thing." So in order to set forth the truth of this revelation in all its fullness, the teacher develops it in the following way:

For the salvation of the soul, first of all true faith is necessary. Holy Scripture states, "Without faith it is impossible to please God" (Heb. 6:6). He who has not faith will be judged. But from the same Holy Scriptures one can see that man cannot himself bring to birth in him faith even as a grain of mustard seed; that faith does not come from us, since it is the gift of God; that faith is a spiritual gift. It is given by the Holy Spirit. That being so, what is to be done? How is one to reconcile man's need of faith with the impossibility of producing it from the human side? The way to do this is revealed in the same Holy Scriptures: "Ask, and it shall be given you." The Apostles could not of themselves arouse the perfection of faith within them, but they prayed to Jesus Christ, "Lord, increase our faith." There you have an example of obtaining faith. It shows that faith is attained by prayer. For the salvation of the soul, besides true faith, good works are also required, for "Faith, if it hath not works, is dead." For man is judged by his works and not by faith alone. "If thou wilt enter into life, keep the commandments: Do not kill, do not commit adultery; do not steal; do not bear false witness; honor thy father and mother; love thy neighbor as thyself." And all these commandments are required to be kept together. "For whosoever shall keep the whole law, and yet offend in one point, he is guilty of all" (James 2:10). So the Apostle James teaches. And the Apostle Paul, describing human weakness, says: "By the deeds of the law there shall no flesh be justified" (Rom. 3:20). "For we know that the law is spiritual; but I am carnal, sold under sin....For to will is present with me, but how to perform that which is good I find not....But the evil which I would not, that I do....With the mind I myself serve the law of God; but with the flesh the law of sin" (Rom. 7). How are the required works of the law of God to be fulfilled when man is without strength and has no power to keep the commandments? He has no possibility of doing this until he asks for it, until he prays about it. "Ye have not because ye ask not" (James 4:2) the Apostle says is the cause. And Jesus Christ Himself says: "Without Me ye can do nothing." And on the subject of doing it with Him, He gives this teaching: "Abide in Me and I in you. He that abideth in me and I in him, the same bringeth forth much fruit." But to be in Him means continually to feel His presence, continually to pray in His Name. "If ye shall ask Me anything in My

Name, that will I do." Thus the possibility of doing good works is reached by prayer itself. An example of this is seen in the Apostle Paul himself: Three times he prayed for victory over temptation, bowing the knee before God the Father, that He would give him strength in the inner man, and was at last bidden above all things to pray, and to pray continually about everything.

From what has been said above, it follows that the whole salvation of man depends upon prayer and, therefore, it is primary and necessary, for by it faith is quickened and through it all good works are performed. In a word, with prayer everything goes forward successfully; without it, no act of Christian piety can be done. Thus, the condition that it should be offered unceasingly and always belongs exclusively to prayer. For the other Christian virtues, each of them has its own time. But in the case of prayer, uninterrupted, continuous action is commanded. Pray without ceasing. It is right and fitting to pray always, to pray everywhere. True prayer has its conditions. It should be offered with a pure mind and heart, with burning zeal, with close attention, with fear and reverence, and with the deepest humility. But what conscientious person would not admit that he is far from fulfilling those conditions, that he offers his prayer more from necessity, more by constraint upon himself than by inclination, enjoyment, and love of it? About this, too, Holy Scripture says that it is not in the power of man to keep his mind steadfast, to cleanse it from unseemly thoughts, for the "thoughts of man are evil from his youth," and that God alone gives us another heart and a new spirit, for "both to will and to do are of God." The Apostle Paul himself says: "My spirit [that is, my voice] prayeth, but my understanding is unfruitful" (1 Cor. 14:14). "We know not what we should pray for as we ought" (Rom. 8:26), the same writer asserts. From this it follows that we in ourselves are unable to offer true prayer. We cannot in our prayers display its essential properties.

Such being the powerlessness of every human being, what remains possible for the salvation of the soul from the side of human will and strength? Man cannot acquire faith without prayer; the same applies to good works. And finally, even to pray purely is not within his power. What, then, is left for him to do? What scope remains for the exercise of his freedom and his strength, so that he may not perish but be saved?

Every action has its quality, and this quality God has reserved to His own will and gift. In order that the dependence of man upon God, the will of God, may be shown the more clearly, and that he may be plunged more deeply into humility, God has assigned to the will and strength of man only the quantity of prayer. He has commanded unceasing prayer, always to pray, at all times and in every place. By this the secret method of achieving true prayer, and at the same time faith, and the fulfillment of God's commandments, and salvation, are revealed. Thus, it is quantity which is assigned to man, as his share; frequency of prayer is his own, and within the province of his will. This is exactly what the Fathers of the Church teach. St. Macarius the Great says truly to pray is the gift of grace. Isikhi says that frequency of prayer becomes a habit and turns into second nature, and without frequent calling upon the Name of Jesus Christ it is impossible to cleanse the heart. The Venerable Callistus and Ignatius counsel frequent, continuous prayer in the Name of Jesus Christ before all ascetic exercises and good works, because frequency brings even the imperfect prayer to perfection. Blessed Diadokh asserts that if a man calls upon the Name of God as often as possible, then he will not fall into sin. What experience and wisdom there are here, and how near to the heart these practical instructions of the Fathers are. In their experience and simplicity they throw much light upon the means of bringing the soul to perfection. What a sharp contrast with the moral instructions of the theoretical reason! Reason argues thus: Do such and such good actions, arm yourself with courage, use the strength of your will, persuade yourself by considering the happy results of virture--for example, cleanse the mind and the heart from worldly dreams, fill their place with instructive meditations; do good and you will be respected and be at peace, live in the way that your reason and conscience require. But alas! With all its strength, all that does not attain its purpose without frequent prayer, without summoning the help of God.

Now let us go on to some further teaching of the Fathers, and we shall see what they say, for example, about purifying the soul. St. John of the Ladder writes: "When the spirit is darkened by unclean thoughts, put the enemy to flight by the Name of Jesus repeated frequently. A more powerful and effective weapon than this you will not find, in heaven or on earth." St. Gregory the Sinaite teaches thus: "Know this, that no one can control his mind by himself, and, therefore, at a time of unclean thoughts call upon the Name of Jesus Christ often and at frequent intervals, and the thoughts will be quieted down." How simple and easy a method! Yet it is tested by experience. What a contrast with the counsel of the theoretical reason, which presumptuously strives to attain purity by its own efforts.

Noting these instructions based upon the experience of the Holy Fathers we pass on the real conclusion: that the principal, the only, and a very easy method of reaching the goal of salvation and spiritual perfection is the frequency and the uninterruptedness of prayer, however feeble it may be. Christian soul, if you do not find within yourself the power to worship God in spirit and in truth, if your heart still feels no warmth and sweet satisfaction in mental and interior prayer, then bring to the sacrifice of prayer what you can, what lies within the scope of your will, what is within your power. Let the humble instrument of your lips first of all grow familiar with frequent persistent prayerful invocation. Let them call upon the mighty Name of Jesus Christ often and without interruption. This is not a great labor and is within the power of everyone. This, too, is what the precept of the Holy Apostle enjoins: "By Him, therefore, let us offer the sacrifice of praise to God continually, that is, the fruit of our lips, giving thanks to His Name" (Heb. 8:5).

Frequency of prayer certainly forms a habit and becomes second nature. It brings the mind and the heart into a proper state from time to time. Suppose a man continually fulfills this one commandment of God about ceaseless prayer, then in that one thing he would have fulfilled all; for if he uninterruptedly, at all times, and in all circumstances, offers the prayer, calling in secret upon the most Holy Name of Jesus (although at first he may do so without spiritual ardor and zeal and even forcing himself), then he will have no time for vain conversation, for judging his neighbors, for useless waste of time in sinful pleasures of the senses. Every evil thought of his would meet opposition to its growth. Every sinful act he contemplated would not come to fruition so readily as with an empty mind. Much talking and vain talking would be checked or entirely done away with, and every fault at once cleansed from the soul by the gracious power of so frequently calling upon the Divine Name. The frequent exercise of prayer would often recall the soul from sinful action and summon it to what is the essential exercise of its skill, to union with God. Now do you see how important and necessary quantity is in prayer? Frequency in prayer is the one method of attaining pure and true prayer. It is the very best and most effective preparation for prayer, and the surest way of reaching the goal of prayer, and salvation.

To convince yourself finally about the necessity and fruitfulness of frequent prayer, note (1) that every impulse and every thought of prayer is the work of the Holy Spirit and the voice of your guardian angel; (2) that the Name of Jesus Christ invoked in prayer contains in itself self-existent and self-acting salutary power, and therefore, (3) do not be disturbed by the imperfection or dryness of your prayer, and await with patience the fruit of frequently calling upon the Divine Name. Do not listen to the inexperienced, thoughtless insinuation of the vain world that lukewarm invocation, even if it be importunate, is useless repetition. No; the power of the Divine Name and the frequent calling upon it will reveal its fruit in its season. A certain spiritual writer has spoken very beautifully about this. "I know," he says, "that to many so-called spiritual and wise philosophers, who search everywhere for sham greatness and practices that are noble in the eyes of reason and pride, the simple, vocal, but frequent exercise of prayer appears of little significance, as a lowly occupation, even a mere trifle. But, unhappy ones, they deceive themselves, and they forget the teaching of Jesus Christ: 'Except ye be converted and become as little children, ye shall not enter into the kingdom of heaven' (Matt. 18:3). They work out for themselves a sort of science of prayer, on the unstable foundations of the natural reason. Do we require much learning or thought or knowledge to say with a pure heart, 'Jesus, Son of God, have mercy on me'? Does not our Divine Teacher Himself praise such frequent prayer? Ah, Christian soul, pluck up your courage and do not silence the unbroken invocations of your prayer, although it may be that this cry of yours comes from a heart which is still at war with itself and half filled by the world. Never mind! Only go on with it and don't let it be silenced and don't be disturbed. It will itself purify itself by repetition. Never let your memory lose hold of this: 'Greater is He that is in you than he that is in the world' (1 John 1:4). 'God is greater than our heart, and knoweth all things,' says the Apostle.

And so after all these convincing arguments that frequent prayer, so powerful in all human weakness, is certainly attainable by man and lies fully within his own will, make up your mind to try, even if only for a single day at first. Maintain a watch over yourself and make the frequency of your prayer such that far more time is occupied in the twenty-four hours with the prayerful calling upon the Name of Jesus Christ than with other matters. And this triumph of prayer over worldly affairs will in time certainly show you that this day has not been lost, but has been secured for salvation; that in the scales of the divine judgment frequent prayer outweighs your weakness and evildoing, and blots out the sins of that day in the memorial book of conscience; that it sets your feet upon the ladder of righteousness and gives you hope of sanctification in the life to come[24].

The Pilgrim. With all my heart I thank you, Holy Father. With that reading of yours you have given

---

[24] The original has a note here as follows: "from the author's MS received by Father Ambrose of the Dobry Monastery."

pleasure to my sinful soul. For the love of God, be so kind as to allow me to copy out for myself what you have read. I can do it in an hour or two. Everything you read was so beautiful and comforting and is so understandable and clear to my stupid mind, like the *Philokalia*, in which the Holy Fathers treat the same subject. Here, for instance, John Karpathisky in the fourth part of the *Philokalia* also says that if you have not the strength for self-control and ascetic achievements, then know that God is willing to save you by prayer. But how beautifully and understandably all that is drawn out in your notebook. I thank God first of all, and then you, that I have been allowed to hear it.

The Professor. I also listened with great attention and pleasure to your reading, Reverend Father. All arguments, when they rest upon strict logic, are a delight to me. But at the same time it seems to me that they make the possibility of continual prayer in a high degree dependent on circumstances which are favorable to it and upon entirely quiet solitude. For I agree that frequent and ceaseless prayer is a powerful and unique means of obtaining the help of divine grace in all acts of devotion for the sanctifying of the soul, and that it is within the power of man. But this method can be used only when man avails himself of the possibility of solitude and quiet. In getting away from business and worries and distractions he can pray frequently or even continually. He then has to contend only with sloth or with the tedium of his own thoughts. But if he is bound by duties and by constant business, if he necessarily finds himself in a noisy company of people, and has an earnest desire to pray often, he cannot carry out this desire because of the inevitable distractions. Consequently the one method of frequent prayer, since it is dependent upon favorable circumstances, cannot be used by everybody, nor belong to all.

The Skhimnik. It is no use drawing a conclusion of that kind. Not to mention the fact that the heart which has been taught interior prayer can always pray and call upon the Name of God unhindered during any occupation, whether of the body or the mind, and in any noise (those who know this know it from experience, and those who do not know it must be taught by gradual training), one can confidently say that no outward distraction can interrupt prayer in one who wishes to pray, for the secret thought of man does not depend upon any link with external environment and is entirely free in itself. It can at all times be perceived and directed toward prayer; even the very tongue can secretly without outward sound express prayer in the presence of many people and during external occupations. Besides, our business is surely not so important and our conversation so interesting that it is impossible during them to find a way at times of frequently calling upon the Name of Jesus Christ, even if the mind has not yet been trained to continuous prayer. Although, of course, solitude and escape from distracting things does constitute the chief condition for attentive and continuous prayer, still we ought to feel ourselves to blame for the rarity of our prayer, because the amount and frequency is under the control of everybody, both the healthy and the sick. It does lie within the scope of his will. Instances which prove this are to be found in those who, although burdened by obligations, distracting duties, cares, worries, and work, have not only always called upon the divine Name of Jesus Christ, but even in this way learned and attained the ceaseless inward Prayer of the Heart. Thus the Patriarch Photius, who was called to the Patriarchal dignity from among the ranks of the senators, while governing the vast diocese of Constantinople, persevered continually in the invocation of the Name of God, and thus attained even the self-acting Prayer of the Heart. Thus Callistus on the Holy Mount Athos learned ceaseless prayer while carrying on his busy life as a cook. So the simple-hearted Lazarus, burdened with continual work for the brotherhood, uninterruptedly, in the midst of all his noisy occupations, repeated the Jesus Prayer and was at peace. And many others similarly have practiced the continuous invocation of the Name of God.

If it were an impossible thing to pray amidst distracting business or in the society of other people, then, of course, it would not have been bidden us. St. John Chrysostom, in his teaching about prayer, speaks as follows: "No one should give the answer that it is impossible for a man occupied with worldly cares, and who is unable to go to Church, to pray always. Everywhere, wherever you may find yourself, you can set up an Altar[25] to God in your mind by means of prayer. And so it is fitting to pray at your trade, on a journey, standing at the counter, or sitting at your handicraft. Everywhere and in every place it is possible to pray, and, indeed, if a man diligently turns his attention upon himself, then everywhere he will find convenient circumstances for prayer, if only he is convinced of the fact that prayer should constitute his chief occupation and come before every other duty. And in that case he would, of course, order his affairs with

---

[25] Altar. In Orthodox churches, "Altar" is the name given to that part of the building which is known in the West as the "Sanctuary." What Westerners call the "Altar" is in known in the East as the "Throne" or "Holy Table." In Orthodox phraseology the Throne is said to stand within the Altar.

greater decision; in necessary conversation with other people he would maintain brevity, a tendency to silence, and a disinclination for useless words; he would not be unduly anxious about worrying things. And in all these ways he would find more time for quiet prayer. In such an order of life all his actions, by the power of the invocation of the Name of God, would be signalized by success, and finally he would train himself to the uninterrupted prayerful invocation of the Name of Jesus Christ. He would come to know from experience that frequency of prayer, this sole means of salvation, is a possibility for the will of man, that it is possible to pray at all times, in all circumstances, and in every place, and easily to rise from frequent vocal prayer to prayer of the mind and from that to Prayer of the Heart, which opens up the Kingdom of God within us.

The Professor. I agree that during mechanical occupations it is possible and even easy to pray frequently, even continuously; for mechanical bodily work does not require profound exercise of the mind or great consideration, and, therefore, while it is going on my mind can be immersed in continuous prayer and my lips follow in the same way. But if I have to be occupied with something exclusively intellectual, as, for instance, attentive reading, or thinking out some deep matter, or literary composition, how can I pray with mind and my lips in such a case? And since prayer is above all things an action of the mind, how, at one and the same time, can I give one and the same mind different sorts of things to do?

The Skhimnik. The solution of your problem is not at all difficult, if we take into consideration that people who pray continually are divided into three classes. First, the beginners; secondly, those who have made some progress; and thirdly, the fully trained. Now, the beginners are frequently capable of experiencing at times an impulse of the mind and heart toward God and of repeating short prayers with the lips, even while engaged in mental work. Those who have made some progress and reached a certain stability of mind are able to occupy themselves with meditation or writing in the uninterrupted presence of God as the basis of prayer. The following example will illustrate this. Imagine that a severe and exacting monarch ordered you to compose a treatise on some abstruse subject in his presence, at the steps of his throne. Although you might be absolutely occupied by your work, the presence of the king who has power over you and who holds your life in his hands would still not allow you to forget a single moment that you are thinking, considering, and writing, not in solitude, but in a place which demands of you particular reverence, respect, and decorum. This lively feeling of the nearness of the king very clearly expresses the possibility of being occupied in ceaseless inward prayer even during intellectual work. So far as the others are concerned, those who by long custom or by the mercy of God have progressed from prayer of the mind and reached Prayer of the Heart, they do no break off their continuous prayer during profound mental exercises, nor even during sleep itself. As the All Wise has told us, "I sleep, but my heart waketh" (Cant. 5:2). Many, that is, who have achieved this mechanism of the heart acquire such an aptitude for calling upon the Divine Name that it will of itself arouse itself to prayer, incline the mind and the whole spirit to a flood of ceaseless prayer in whatever condition the one who prays finds himself, and however abstract and intellectual his occupation at the time.

The Pilgrim Continues His Way

The Priest. Allow me, Reverend Father, to say what is in my mind. Let me have a turn and say a word or two. It was admirably put in the article you read that the one means of salvation and of reaching perfection is frequency of prayer, of whatever sort. Now, I do not very easily understand that, and it appears to me like this. What would be the use if I pray and invoke the Name of God continually with my tongue only and pay no attention to, and do not understand, what I am saying? That would be nothing but vain repetition. The result of it will only be that the tongue will go chattering on, and the mind, hindered in its meditations by this, will have its activity impaired. God does not ask for words, but for an attentive mind and a pure heart. Would it not be better to offer a prayer, be it only a short one, even rarely may be, or only at stated times, but with attention, with zeal and warmth of heart, and with due understanding? Otherwise, although you may say the prayer day and night, yet you have not got purity of mind, you are not performing a work of devotion, not achieving anything for your salvation. You are relying upon nothing but outward chatter, and you get tired and bored, and in the end the result is that your faith in prayer is completely chilled and you throw over altogether this fruitlessness proceeding. Further, the uselessness of prayer with the lips only can be seen from what is revealed to us in Holy Scripture, as, for instance, "This people draweth nigh unto Me with their mouth and honoreth Me with their lips, but their heart is far from Me" (Matt. 15:8). "Not everyone that saith unto Me, Lord, Lord, shall enter into the kingdom of Heaven" (Matt. 7:21). "I had rather speak five words with my understanding...than ten thousand words in an unknown tongue" (1 Cor. 14:19). All this shows the fruitlessness of outward inattentive prayer with the mouth.

The Skhimnik. There might be something in your point of view if, with the advise to pray with the mouth, there were not added the need for it to be continuous; if prayer in the Name of Jesus Christ did not possess self-acting power and did not win for itself attention and zeal as a result of continuity in the exercise. But as the matter now in question is frequency, length of time, and uninterruptedness of prayer (although it may be carried on at first inattentively or with dryness), then, on account of this very fact, the conclusions that you mistakenly draw come to nothing. Let us look into the matter a little more closely. One spiritual writer, after arguing the very great value and fruitfulness of frequent prayer expressed in one form of words, says finally, "Many so-called enlightened people regard this frequent offering of one and the same prayer as useless and even trifling, calling it mechanical and a thoughtless occupation of simple people. But unfortunately they do not know the secret which is revealed as a result of this mechanical exercise; they do not know how this frequent service of the lips imperceptibly becomes a genuine appeal of the heart, sinks down into the inward life, becomes a delight, becomes, as it were, natural to the soul, bringing it light and nourishment and leading it on to union with God." It seems to me that these censorious people are like those little children who were being taught the alphabet and how to read. When they got tired of it they cried out, "Would it not be a hundred times better to go fishing, like father, than to spend the whole day in ceaselessly repeating a, b, c,, or scrawling on a sheet of paper with a pen?" The value of being able to read and the enlightenment which it brings, which they could have only as a result of this wearisome

The Pilgrim Continues His Way

learning the letters by heart, was a hidden secret to them. In the same way the simple and frequent calling upon the Name of God is a hidden secret to those people who are not persuaded of its results and its very great value. They, estimating the act of faith by the strength of their own inexperienced and shortsighted reason, forget in so doing that man has two natures, in direct influence one upon another, that man is made of body and soul. Why, for example, when you desire to purify your soul, do your first of all deal with your body, make it fast, deprive it of nourishment and stimulating food? It is, of course, in order that it may not hinder, or, to put it better, so that it may be the means of promoting purity of soul and enlightenment of mind, so that the continual feeling of bodily hunger may remind you of your resolution to seek for inward perfection and the things pleasing to God, which you so easily forget. And you find by experience that through the outward fast of your body you achieve the inward refining of your mind, the peace of your heart, an instrument for the taming of your passions, and a reminder of spiritual effort. And thus, by means of outward and material things, you receive inward and spiritual profit and help. You must understand the same thing about frequent prayer with the lips, which by its long duration draws out the inward Prayer of the Heart and promotes unity of the mind with God. It is vain to imagine that the tongue, wearied by this frequency and barren lack of understanding, will be obliged to give up entirely this outward effort of prayer as useless. No, experience here shows us exactly the opposite. Those who have practiced ceaseless prayer assure us that what happens is this: One who has made up his mind to call without ceasing upon the Name of Jesus Christ or, what is the same thing, to say the Jesus Prayer continuously, at first of course, finds difficulty and has to struggle

194

against sloth. But the longer and the harder he works at it, the more he grows familiar with the task imperceptibly, so that in the end the lips and the tongue acquire such capacity for moving themselves that even without any effort on his part they themselves act irresistibly and say that Prayer voicelessly. At the same time the mechanism of the throat muscles is so trained that in praying he begins to feel that the saying of the prayer is a perpetual and essential property of himself, and even feels every time he stops as though something were missing in him. And so it results from this that his mind in its turn begins to yield, to listen to this involuntary action of the lips, and is aroused by it to attention which in the end becomes a source of delight to the heart, and true prayer.

There you see the true and beneficent effect of continuous or frequent vocal prayer, exactly the opposite of what people who have neither tried nor understood it suppose. Concerning those passages in Holy Scripture which you brought forward in support of your objection, these are to be explained, if we make a proper examination of them. Hypocritical worship of God with the mouth, ostentation about it, or insincere praise in the cry, "Lord, Lord," Jesus Christ exposed for this reason, that the faith of the proud Pharisees was a matter of the mouth only, and in no degree did their conscience justify their faith, nor did they acknowledge it in their heart. It was to them that these things were said, and they do not refer to saying prayers, about which Jesus Christ gave direct, explicit, and definite instructions. "Men ought always to pray and not to faint." Similarly, when the Apostle Paul says he prefers five words spoken with the understanding to a multitude of words without thought or in an unknown tongue in the Church, he is speaking about teaching in general, not about prayer in particular, on which subject he firmly says, "I will therefore that men pray everywhere" (1 Tim. 2:8), and his is the general precept, "Pray without ceasing" (1 Thess. 5:17). Do you now see how fruitful frequent prayer is, for all its simplicity, and what serious consideration the proper understanding of Holy Scripture requires?

The Pilgrim. Truly it is so, Reverend Father. I have seen many who quite simply, without the light of any education whatever and not even knowing what attention is, offer the Prayer of Jesus with their mouths unceasingly. I have known them to reach a stage when their lips and tongue could not be restrained from saying The Prayer. It brought them such happiness and enlightenment, and changed them from weak and negligent people into podvizhniki and champions of virtue.[26]

The Skhimnik. Prayer brings a man to a new birth, as it were. Its power is so great that nothing, no degree of suffering will stand against it. If you like, by way of

---

[26] The original has a note here as follows: "In the nineties of the last century there died at the Troitskaya Lavra a Starets, a layman in his 108th year; he could not read or write, but he said the Jesus Prayer even during his sleep, and lived continually as the child of God, with a heart that yearned for Him. His name was Gordi." Troitskaya Lavra is the famous Monastery of the Holy Trinity near Moscow, founded by St. Sergei in the fourteenth century. The part it played in Russian religious life has been compared by Frere in some respects to the Cluniac movement (Links in the Chain of Russian Church History, p.36). The Troitskaya Lavra was intimately connected with Russian history, and was the focal point of the national movement which drove out the Poles and placed the first Romanov on the Russian throne in 1613.

The Pilgrim Continues His Way

saying good-bye, brothers, I will read you a short but interesting article which I have with me.

All. We shall listen with the greatest pleasure.

ON THE POWER OF PRAYER

The Skhimnik. Prayer is so powerful, so mighty, that "pray, and do what you like." Prayer will guide you to right and just action. In order to please God nothing more is needed than love. "Love, and do what you will," says the Blessed Augustine, "for he who truly loves cannot wish to do anything which is not pleasing to the one he loves." Since prayer is the outpouring and the activity of love, then one can truly say of it similarly, "Nothing more is needed for salvation than continuous prayer." "Pray, and do what you will," and you will reach the goal of prayer. You will gain enlightenment by it.

To draw out our understanding of this matter in more detail, let us take some examples:

1. "Pray, and think what you will." Your thoughts will be purified by prayer. Prayer will give you enlightenment of mind; it will remove and drive away all ill-judged thoughts. This is asserted by St. Gregory the Sinaite. If you wish to drive away thoughts and purify the mind, his counsel is "drive them away by prayer." For nothing can control thoughts as prayer can. St. John of the Ladder also says about this, "Overcome the foes in your mind by the Name of Jesus. You will find no other weapon than this."

197

2. "Pray, and do what you will." Your acts will be pleasing to God and useful and salutary to yourself. Frequent prayer, whatever it may be about, does not remain fruitless, because in it is the power of grace, "for whosoever shall call on the Name of the Lord shall be saved" (Acts 2:21). For example a man who had prayed without success and without devotion was granted through this prayer clearness of understanding and a call to repentance. A pleasure-loving girl prayed on her return home, and the prayer showed her the way to the virgin life and obedience to the teaching of Jesus Christ.

3. "Pray, and do not labor much to conquer your passions by your own strength." Prayer will destroy them in you. "For greater is He that is in you than he that is in the world" (1 John 4:4), says Holy Scripture. And St. John Karpathisky teaches that if you have not the gift of self-control, do not be cast down, but know that God requires of you diligence in prayer and the prayer will save you. The Starets about whom we are told in the Otechnik[27] that, when he fell into sin, did not give way to depression, but betook himself to prayer and by it recovered his balance, is a case in point.

4. "Pray, and fear nothing." Fear no misfortunes, fear no disasters. Prayer will protect you and ward them off. Remember St. Peter, who had little faith and was sinking; St. Paul, who prayed in prison; the Monk who was delivered by prayer from the onset of temptation; the girl who was saved from the evil purpose of a soldier as the result of prayer; and similar cases, which illustrate the power, the might,

---

[27] *Otechnik.* Lives of the Fathers with extracts from their writings.

the universality of prayer in the Name of Jesus Christ.

5. Pray somehow or other, only pray always and be disturbed by nothing. Be light in spirit and peaceful. Prayer will arrange everything and teach you. Remember what the Saints--John Chrysostom and Mark the Ascetic--say about the power of prayer. The first declares that prayer, even though it be offered by us who are full of sin, yet cleanses us at once. The latter says, "To pray somehow is within our power, but to pray purely is the gift of grace." So offer to God what it is within your power to offer. Bring to Him at first just quantity (which is within your power), and God will pour upon you strength in your weakness. "Prayer, dry and distracted maybe, but continuous, will establish a habit and become second nature and turn itself into prayer that is pure, luminous, flaming, and worthy."

6. It is to be noted, finally, that if the time of your vigilance in prayer is prolonged, then naturally no time will be left not only for doing sinful actions but even for thinking of them.

Now, do you see what profound thoughts are focused in that wise saying, "Love, and do what you will"; "Pray, and do what you will"? How comforting and consoling is all this for the sinner overwhelmed by his weakness, groaning under the burden of his warring passions.

Prayer--there you have the whole of what is given to us as the universal means of salvation and of the growth of the soul into perfection. Just that. But when prayer is named, a condition is added. Pray without ceasing is the command of God's Word. Consequently, prayer shows its most effective power and fruit when it is offered often, ceaselessly; for frequency of prayer undoubtedly belongs to our will, just as purity, zeal and perfection in prayer are the gifts of grace.

And so we will pray as often as we can; we will consecrate our whole life to prayer, even if it be subject to distractions to begin with. Frequent practice of it will teach us attentiveness. Quantity will certainly lead on to quality. "If you want to learn to do anything whatever well you must do it as often as possible," said an experienced spiritual writer.

The Professor. Truly prayer is a great matter, and ardent frequency of it is the key to open the treasury of its grace. But how often I find a conflict in myself between ardor and sloth. How glad I should be to find the way to gain the victory and to convince myself and arouse myself to continuous application to prayer.

The Skhimnik. Many spiritual writers offer a number of ways based upon sound reasoning for stimulating diligence in prayer. For example, (1) they advise you to steep your mind in thoughts of the necessity, the excellence, and the fruitfulness of prayer for saving the soul; (2) make yourself firmly convinced that God absolutely requires prayer of us and that His Word everywhere commands it; (3) always remember that if you are slothful and careless about prayer you can make no progress in acts of devotion nor in attaining peace and salvation and, therefore, will inevitably suffer both punishment on earth and torment in the life to come; and (4) enhearten your resolution by the example of the

The Pilgrim Continues His Way

Saints who all attained holiness and salvation by the way of continuous prayer.

Although all these methods have their value and arise from genuine understanding, yet the pleasure-loving soul which is sick with listlessness, even when it has accepted and used them, rarely sees the fruit of them, for this reason: these medicines are bitter to its impaired sense of taste and too weak for its deeply injured nature. For what Christian is there who does not know that he ought to pray often and diligently, that God requires it of him, that we are punished for sloth in prayer, that all the Saints have ardently and constantly prayed? Nevertheless, how rarely does all this knowledge show good results. Every observer of himself sees that he justifies but little, and but rarely, these promptings of reason and conscience, and through infrequent remembrance of them lives all the while in the same bad and slothful way. And so, in their experience and godly wisdom, the Holy Fathers, knowing the weakness of will and the exaggerated love of pleasure in the heart of man, take a special line about it, and in this respect put jam with the powder and smear the edge of the medicine cup with honey. They show the easiest and most effective means of doing away with sloth and indifference in prayer, in the hope, with God's help, of attaining by prayer perfection and the sweet expectation of love for God.

They advise you to meditate as often as possible about the state of your soul and to read attentively what the Fathers have written on the subject. They give encouraging assurance that these enjoyable inward feelings may be readily and easily attained in prayer, and say how much they are to be desired. Heartfelt delight, a flood of inward warmth and light, ineffable enthusiasm, joy, lightness of heart, profound peace, and the very essence of blessedness and happy content are all results of prayer in the heart. By steeping itself in such reflections as these, the weak cold soul is kindled and strengthened, it is encouraged by ardor for prayer and is, as it were, enticed to put the practice of prayer to the test. As St. Isaac the Syrian says, "Joy is an enticement to the soul, joy which is the outcome of hope blossoming in the heart, and meditation upon its hope is the well-being of the heart."

The same writer continues: "At the outset of this activity and right to the end there is presupposed some sort of method and hope for its completion, and this both arouses the mind to lay a foundation for the task and from the vision of its goal the mind borrows consolation during the labor of reaching it." In the same way St. Isikhi, after describing the hindrance that sloth is to prayer and clearing away misconceptions about the renewal of ardor for it, finally says outright, "If we are not ready to desire the silence of the heart for any other reason, then let it be for the delightful feeling of it in the soul and for the gladness that it brings." It follows from this that this Father gives the enjoyable feeling of gladness as an incitement to assiduity in prayer, and in the same way St. Macarius the Great teaches that our spiritual efforts (prayer) should be carried out with the purpose and in the hope of producing fruit--that is, enjoyment in our hearts. Clear instances of the potency of this method are to be seen in very many passages of the *Philokalia*, which contains detailed descriptions of the delights of prayer. One who is struggling with the infirmity of sloth or dryness in prayer ought to read them over as often as possible, considering himself, however, unworthy of these enjoyments and ever reproaching himself for negligence in prayer.

The Priest. Will not such meditation lead the inexperienced person to spiritual voluptuousness, as the theologians call that tendency of the soul which is greedy of excessive consolation and sweetness of grace, and is not content to fulfill the work of devotion from a sense of obligation and duty without dreaming about reward?

The Professor. I think that the theologians in this case are warning men against excess or greed of spiritual happiness, and are not entirely rejecting enjoyment and consolation in virtue. For if the desire for reward is not perfection, nevertheless God has not forbidden man to think about rewards and consolation, and even Himself uses the idea of reward to incite men to fulfill His commandments and to attain perfection. "Honor thy father and thy mother." There is the command and you see the reward follows as a spur to its fulfillment, "and it shall be well with thee." "If thou wilt be perfect, go, sell, all that thou hast and come and follow Me." There is the demand for perfection, and immediately upon it comes the reward as an inducement to attain perfection, "and thou shalt have treasure in heaven. Blessed are ye when men shall hate you, and when they shall separate you from their company, and shall reproach you, and cast out your name as evil, for the Son of man's sake" (Luke 6:22). There is a great demand for a spiritual achievement which needs unusual strength of soul and unshakable patience. And so for that there is a great reward and consolation, which are able to arouse and maintain this unusual strength of soul-- "For your reward is great in heaven." For this reason I think that a certain desire for enjoyment in Prayer of the Heart is necessary and probably constitutes the means of attaining both diligence and success in it. And so all this undoubtedly supports the practical teaching on this subject which we have just heard from the skhimnik.

The Skhimnik. One of the great theologians--that is to say, St. Macarius of Egypt--speaks in the clearest possible way about this matter. He says, "As when you are planting a vine you bestow your thought and labor with the purpose of gathering the vintage, and if you do not, all your labor will be useless, so also in prayer, if you do not look for spiritual fruit--that is, love, peace, joy, and the rest--your labor will be useless. And, therefore, we ought to fulfill our spiritual duties (prayer) with the purpose and hope of gathering fruit--that is to say, comfort and enjoyment in our hearts." Do you see how clearly the Holy Father answers this question about the need for enjoyment in prayer? And, as a matter of fact, there has just come into my mind a point of view which I read not long ago of a writer on spiritual things, to this effect: that the naturalness of prayer to man is the chief cause of his inclination toward it. So the examination of this naturalness, in my opinion, may also serve as a potent means of arousing diligence in prayer, the means which the professor is so eagerly looking for.

Let me now sum up shortly some points I drew attention to in that notebook. For instance, the writer says that reason and nature lead man to the knowledge of God. The first investigates the fact that there cannot be action without cause, and ascending the ladder of tangible things from the lower to the higher, at last reaches the First Cause, God. The second displays at every step its marvelous wisdom, harmony, order, gradation, gives the basic material for the ladder which leads from finite causes to the infinite. Thus, the natural man arrives naturally at the knowledge of God. And, therefore, there is not, and never has been, any people, any barbarous tribe, without some knowledge of God. As a result of this knowledge the most savage islander, without any impulse from outside, as it were involuntarily raises his gaze to heaven, falls on his knees, breathes out a sigh which he does not understand, necessary as it is, and has a direct feeling that there is something which draws him upward, something urging him toward the unknown. From this foundation all natural religions arise. And in this connection it is very remarkable that universally the essence or the soul of every religion consists in secret prayer, which shows itself in some form of movement of the spirit and what is clearly an oblation, though more or less distorted by the darkness of the coarse and wild understanding of heathen people. The more surprising this fact is in the eyes of reason, the greater is the demand upon us to discover the hidden cause of this wonderful thing which finds expression in a natural movement toward prayer. The psychological answer to this is not difficult to find. The root, the head, and the strength of all passions and actions in man is his innate love of self. The deep-rooted and universal idea of self-preservation clearly confirms this. Every human wish, every undertaking, every action has as its purpose the satisfaction of self-love, the seeking of the man's own happiness. The satisfaction of this demand accompanies the natural man all through his life. But the human spirit is not satisfied with anything that belongs to the senses, and the innate love of self never abates its urgency. And so desires develop more and more, the endeavor to attain happiness grows stronger, fills the imagination, and incites the feelings to this same end. The flood of this inward feeling and desire as it develops is the natural arousing to prayer. It is a requirement of self-love which attains its purpose with difficulty. The less the natural man succeeds in attaining happiness and the more he has it in view, the more his longing grows and the more he finds an outlet for it in prayer. He betakes himself in petition for what he desires to the unknown cause of all being. So it is that innate self-love, the principal element in life, is a deep-seated stimulus to prayer in the natural man. The all-wise Creator of all things has imbued the nature of man with a capacity for self-love precisely as an "enticement," to use the expression of the Fathers, which will draw the fallen being of man upward into touch with celestial things. Oh! if man had not spoiled this capacity, if only he had kept it in its excellence, in touch with his spiritual nature! Then he would have had a powerful incentive and an effective means of bringing him along the road to moral perfection. But, alas! how often he makes of this noble capacity a base passion of self-love when he turns it into an instrument of his animal nature.

The Starets. I thank you from my heart, all my dear visitors. Your salutary conversation has been a great consolation to me and taught me, in my experience, many profitable things. May God give you His grace in return for your edifying love.

(They all separate.)

Chapter III

The Pilgrim. My devout friend the professor and I could not resist our desire to start on our journey, and before doing so to look in and say a last good-bye to you and ask for your prayers.

The Professor. Yes, our intimacy with you has meant a great deal to us, and so have the salutary conversations on spiritual things which we have enjoyed at your house in company with your friends. We shall keep the memory of all this in our hearts as a pledge of fellowship and Christian love in that distant land to which we are hastening.

The Starets. Thank you for remembering me. And, by the way, how opportune your arrival is. There are two travelers stopping with me, a Moldavian Monk and a hermit who has lived in silence for twenty-five years in a forest. They want to see you. I will call them at once. Here they are.

The Pilgrim. Ah, how blessed a life of solitude is! And how suitable for bringing the soul into unbroken union with God! The silent forest is like a garden of Eden in which the delightful tree of life grows in the prayerful heart of the recluse. If I had something to live on, nothing, I think, would keep me from the life of a hermit!

The Professor. Everything seems particularly desirable to us from a distance. But we all find out by experience that every place, though it may have its advantages, has its drawbacks too. Of course, if one is melancholy by temperament and inclined to silence, then a solitary life is a comfort. But what a lot of

207

dangers lie along that road. The history of the ascetic life provides many instances to show that numbers of recluses and hermits, having entirely deprived themselves of human society, have fallen into self-deception and profound seductions.

The Hermit. I am surprised at how often one hears it said in Russia, not only in religious houses, but even among God-fearing layfolk, that many who desire the hermit life, or exercise in the practice of interior prayer, are held back from following up this inclination by the fear that seductions will ruin them. Insisting on this, they bring forward instances of the conclusion their minds have arrived at as a reason alike for avoiding the interior life themselves and for keeping other people from it also. To my mind this arises from two causes: either from failure to understand the task and lack of spiritual enlightenment, or from their own indifference to contemplative achievement and jealousy lest others who are at a low level in comparison with themselves should outdistance them in this higher knowledge. It is a great pity that those who hold this conviction do not investigate the teaching of the Holy Fathers on the matter, for they very decidedly teach that one ought neither to fear nor to doubt when one calls upon God. If certain of them have indeed fallen into self-deception and fanaticism, that was the result of pride, of not having a director, and of taking appearances and imagination for reality. Should such a time of testing occur, they continue, it would lead to experience and a crown of glory, for the help of God comes swiftly to protect when such a thing is permitted. Be courageous. "I am with you, fear not," says Jesus Christ. And it follows from this that to feel fear and alarm at the interior life on the pretext of the risk of self-deception is a vain thing. For humble consciousness of one's sins, openness of soul with one's director, and "formlessness" in prayer are a strong and safe defense against those tempting illusions of which many feel so great a fear and, therefore, do not embark upon activity of the mind. Incidentally, these very people find themselves exposed to temptation, as the wise words of Philotheus the Sinaite tell us. He says, "There are many Monks who do not understand the illusion of their own minds, which they suffer at the hands of demons--that is to say, they give themselves diligently to only one form of activity, 'outward good works'; whereas of the mind--that is, of inward contemplation--they have little care, since they are unenlightened and ignorant about this." "Even if they hear of others that grace works inwardly within them, through jealously they regard it as self-deception," St. Gregory the Sinaite declares.

The Professor. Allow me to ask you a question. Of course the consciousness of one's sins is proper for everyone who pays any attention to himself. But how does one proceed when no director is available to guide one in the way of the interior life from his own experience, and when one has opened one's heart to him, to impart to one correct and trustworthy knowledge about the spiritual life? In that case, no doubt, it would be better not to attempt contemplation rather than try it on one's own without a guide. Further, for my part, I don't readily understand how, if one puts oneself in the presence of God, it is possible to observe complete "formlessness." It is not natural, for our soul or our mind can present nothing to the imagination without form, in absolute formlessness. And why, indeed, when the mind is steeped in God, should we not present to the imagination Jesus Christ, or the Holy Trinity, and so on?

The Pilgrim Continues His Way

The Hermit. The guidance of a director or Starets who is experienced and knowledgeable in spiritual things, to whom one can open one's heart every day without hindrance, with confidence and advantage, and tell one's thoughts and what one has met with on the path of interior schooling, is the chief condition for the practice of Prayer of the Heart by one who has entered upon the life of silence. Yet, in cases where it is impossible to find such a one, the same Holy Fathers who prescribe this make an exception. St. Nicephorus the Monk gives clear instructions about it, thus: "During the practice of inward activity of the heart, a genuine and well-informed director is required. If such a one is not at hand, then you must diligently search for one. If you do not find him, then, calling contritely upon God for help, draw instruction and guidance from the teaching of the Holy Fathers and verify it from the Word of God set forth in the Holy Scriptures." Here one must also take into consideration the fact that the seeker of goodwill and zeal can obtain something useful in the way of instruction from ordinary people also. For the Holy Fathers assure us likewise, that if with faith and right intention one questions even a Saracen, he can speak words of value to us. If, on the other hand, one asks for instruction from a prophet, without faith and a righteous purpose, then even he will not satisfy us. We see an instance of this in the case of St. Macarius the Great of Egypt, to whom on one occasion a simple villager gave an explanation that put an end to the distress which he was experiencing.

As regards "formlessness"--that is, not using the imagination and not accepting any sort of vision during contemplation, whether of light, or of an angel, or of Christ, or any Saint, and turning aside from all dreaming-- this, of course, is enjoined by experienced

The Pilgrim Continues His Way

Holy Fathers for this reason: that the power of the imagination may easily incarnate or, so to speak, give life to the representations of the mind, and thus the inexperienced might readily be attracted by these figments, take them as visions of grace, and fall into self-deception, in spite of the fact that Holy Scripture says that Satan himself may assume the form of an angel of light. And that the mind can naturally and easily be in a state of "formlessness" and keep so, even while recollecting the presence of God, can be seen from the fact that the power of the imagination can perceptibly present a thing in "formlessness" and maintain its hold upon such a presentation. Thus, for example, the representation of our souls, of the air, warmth, or cold. When you are cold you can have a lively idea of warmth in your mind, though warmth has no shape, is not an object of sight, and is not measured by the physical feeling of one who finds himself in the cold. In the same way also the presence of the spiritual and incomprehensible being of God may be present to the mind and recognized in the heart in absolute formlessness.

The Pilgrim. During my wanderings I have come across people, devout people who were seeking salvation, who have told me that they were afraid to have anything to do with the interior life, and denounced it as a mere illusion. To several of them I read out of the *Philokalia* the teaching of St. Gregory the Sinaite with some profit. He says that "the action of the heart cannot be an illusion (as that of the mind can), for if the enemy desired to turn the warmth of the heart into his own uncontrolled fire, or to change the gladness of the heart into the dull pleasures of the senses, still time, experience, and the feeling itself would expose his craftiness and cunning, even for those who are not very learned." I have also met other people who, most unhappily, after knowing the way of silence and Prayer of the Heart, have on meeting some obstacle or sinful weakness given way to depression, and given up the inward activity of the heart which they had known.

The Professor. Yes, and that is very natural. I have myself experienced the same thing at times, on occasions when I have lapsed from the interior frame of mind or done something wrong. For since inward Prayer of the Heart is a holy thing and union with God, is it not unseemly and a thing not to be dared to bring a holy thing into a sinful heart, without having first purified it by silent contrite penitence and a proper preparation for communion with God? It is better to be dumb before God than to offer Him thoughtless words out of a heart which is in darkness and distraction.

The Monk. It is a great pity that you think like that. That is despondency, which is the worst of all sins and constitutes the principal weapon of the world of darkness against us. The teaching of our experienced Holy Fathers about this is quite different. St. Nicetas Stethatus says that if you have fallen and sunk down even into the depths of hellish evil, even then you are not to despair, but to turn quickly to God, and He will speedily raise up your fallen heart and give you more strength than you had before. So after every fall and sinful wounding of the heart, the thing to do is immediately to place it in the presence of God for healing and cleansing, just as things that have become infected, if they are exposed for some time to the power of the sun's rays, lose the sharpness and strength of their infection. Many spiritual writers speak positively about this inner conflict with the enemies of salvation, our passions. If you receive wounds a thousand times, still you should by no means give up the life-giving action--that is to say, calling upon Jesus Christ who is present in our hearts. Our actions not only ought not to turn us away from walking in the presence of God and from inward prayer, and so produce disquiet, depression, and sadness in us, but rather further our swift turning to God. The infant who is led by its mother when it begins to walk turns quickly to her and holds on to her firmly when it stumbles.

The Hermit. I look at it in this way, that the spirit of despondency, and agitating and doubting thoughts, are aroused most easily by distraction of the mind and failure to guard the silent resort of one's inner self. The ancient Fathers in their divine wisdom won the victory over despondency and received inward light and strength through hope in God, through peaceful silence and solitude, and they have given us wise and useful counsel: "Sit silently in your cell and it will teach you everything."

The Professor. I have such confidence in you that I listen very gladly to your critical analysis of my thoughts about the silence which you praise so highly, and the benefits of the solitary life which hermits so love to lead. Well, that is what I think: Since all people, by the law of nature ordained by the Creator, are placed in necessary dependence upon one another and, therefore, are bound to help one another in life, to labor for one another, and to be of service to one another, this sociability makes for the well-being of the human race and shows love for one's neighbor. But the silent hermit who has withdrawn from human society, in what way can he, in his inactivity, be of service to his neighbor and what contribution can he make to the well-being of human society? He completely destroys in himself that

213

law of the Creator which concerns union in love of one's kind and beneficent influence upon the brotherhood.

The Hermit. Since this view of yours about silence is incorrect, the conclusion you draw from it will not hold good. Let us consider it in detail. (1) The man who lives in silent solitude is not only not living in a state of inactivity and idleness; he is in the highest degree active, even more than the one who takes part in the life of society. He untiringly acts according to his highest rational nature; he is on guard; he ponders; he keeps his eye upon the state and progress of his moral existence. This is the true purpose of silence. And in the measure that this ministers to his own improvement, it benefits others for whom undistracted submergence within themselves for the development of the moral life is impossible. For he who watches in silence, by communicating his inward experiences either by word (in exceptional cases) or by committing them to writing, promotes the spiritual advantage and the salvation of his brethren. And he does more, and that of a higher kind, than the private benefactor, because the private, emotional charities of people in the world are always limited by the small number of benefits conferred, whereas he who confers benefits by morally attaining to convincing and tested means of perfecting the spiritual life becomes a benefactor of whole peoples. His experience and teaching pass on from generation to generation, as we see ourselves and of which we avail ourselves from ancient times to this day. And this in no sense differs from Christian love; it even surpasses it in its results. (2) The beneficent and most useful influence of the man who observes silence upon his neighbors is not only shown in the communication of his instructive observations upon the interior life, but also the very example of his separated life benefits the attentive layman by leading him to self-knowledge and arousing in him the feeling of reverence. The man who lives in the world, hearing of the devout recluse, or going past the door of his hermitage, feels an impulse to the devout life, has recalled to his mind what man can be upon earth, that it is possible for man to get back to that primitive contemplative state in which he issued from the hands of his Creator. The silent recluse teaches by his very silence, and by his very life he benefits, edifies, and persuades to the search for God. (3) This benefit springs from genuine silence which is illuminated and sanctified by the light of grace. But if the silent one did not have these gifts of grace which make him a light to the world, even if he should have embarked upon the way of silence with the purpose of hiding himself from the society of his kind as the result of sloth and indifference, even then he would confer a great benefit upon the community in which he lives, just as the gardener cuts off dry and barren branches and clears away the weeds so that the growth of the best and most useful may be unimpeded. And this is a great deal. It is of general benefit that the silent one by his seclusion removes the temptations which would inevitably arise from his unedifying life among people and be injurious to the morals of his neighbors.

On the subject of the importance of silence, St. Isaac the Syrian exclaims as follows: "When on one side we place all the actions of this life and on the other silence, we find that it weighs down the scales. Do not place those who perform signs and wonders in the world on a level with those who keep silence with knowledge. Love the inactivity of silence more than the satiety of greedy ones in the world and the turning of many people to God. It is better for you to cut yourself free from the bonds of sin than to liberate slaves from their servitude." Even the most elementary sages have recognized the value of silence. The philosophical school of the Neoplatonists, which embraced many adherents under the guidance of the philosopher Plotinus, developed to a high degree the inner contemplative life which is attained most especially in silence. One spiritual writer said that if the state were developed to the highest degree of education and morals, yet even then it would still be necessary to provide people for contemplation, in addition to the general activities of citizens, in order to preserve the spirit of truth, and having received it from all the centuries that are past, to keep it for the generations to come and hand it on to posterity. Such people, in the Church, are hermits, recluses, and anchorites.

The Pilgrim. I think that no one has so truly valued the excellences of silence as St. John of the Ladder. "Silence," he says, "is the mother of prayer, a return from the captivity of sin, unconscious success in virtue, a continuous ascension to heaven." Yes, and Jesus Christ Himself, in order to show us the advantage and necessity of silent seclusion, often left His public preaching and went into silent places for prayer and quietude. The silent contemplatives are like pillars supporting the devotion of the Church by their secret continuous prayer. Even in the distant past, one sees that many devout layfolk, and even kings and their courtiers, went to visit hermits and men who kept silence in order to ask them to pray for their strengthening and salvation. Thus the silent recluse, too, can serve his neighbor and act to the advantage and the happiness of society by his secluded prayer.

The Pilgrim Continues His Way

The Professor. Now, there again, that is a thought which I do not very easily understand. It is a general custom among all of us Christians to ask for each other's prayers, to want another to pray for me, and to have special confidence in a member of the Church. Is not this simply a demand of self-love? Is it not that we have only caught the habit of saying what we have heard others say, as a sort of fancy of the mind without any serious consideration? Does God require human intercession, since He foresees everything and acts according to His all-blessed providence and not according to our desire, knowing and settling everything before our petition is made, as the Holy Gospel says? Can the prayer of many people really be any stronger to overcome His decisions than the prayer of one person? In that case God would be a respecter of persons. Can the prayer of another person really save me when everybody is commended or put to shame on the ground of his own actions? And, therefore, the request for the prayers of another person is to my mind merely a pious expression of spiritual courtesy, which shows signs of humility and a desire to please by preferring one another, and that is all.

The Monk. If one take only outward considerations into account, and with an elementary philosophy, it might be put in that way. But the spiritual reason blessed by the light of religion and trained by the experiences of the interior life goes a good deal deeper, contemplates more clearly, and in a mystery reveals something entirely different from what you have put forward. So that we may understand this more quickly and clearly, let us take an example and then verify the truth of it from the Word of God. Let us say that a pupil came to a certain teacher for instruction. His feeble capacities and, what is more, his idleness and lack of concentration prevented him from attaining any success in his studies, and they put him in the category of the idle and unsuccessful. Feeling sad at this, he did not know what to do, nor how to contend with his deficiencies. Then he met another pupil, a classmate of his, who was more able than he, more diligent and successful, and he explained his trouble to him. The other took an interest in him and invited him to work with him. "Let us work together," he said, "and we shall be keener, more cheerful and, therefore, more successful." And so they began to study together, each sharing with the other what he understood. The subject of their study was the same. And what followed after several days? The indifferent one became diligent; he came to like his work, his carelessness was changed to ardor and intelligence, which had a beneficial effect upon his character and morals also. And the intelligent one in his turn became more able and industrious. In the effect they had upon one another they arrived at a common advantage. And this is very natural, for man is born in the society of people; he develops his rational understanding through people, habits of life, training, emotions, the action of the will--in a word, everything he receives from the example of his kind. And, therefore, as the life of men consists in the closest relations and the strongest influences of one upon another, he who lives among a certain sort of people becomes accustomed to that kind of habit, behavior, and morals. Consequently the cool become enthusiastic, the stupid become sharp, the idle are aroused to activity by a lively interest in their fellow men. Spirit can give itself to spirit and act beneficially upon another and attract another to prayer, to attention. It can encourage him in despondency, turn him from vice, and arouse him to holy action. And so by helping each other they can become more devout, more energetic spiritually, more reverent. There you have the secret of prayer for others, which explains the devout custom on the part of Christian people of praying for one another and asking for the prayers of the brethren.

And from this one can see that it is not that God is pleased, as the great ones of this world are, by a great many petitions and intercessions, but that the very spirit and power of prayer cleanses and arouses the soul for whom the prayer is offered and presents it ready for union with God. If mutual prayer by those who are living upon earth is so beneficial, then in the same way we may infer that prayer for the departed also is mutually beneficial because of the very close link that exists between the heavenly world and this. In this way souls of the Church Militant can be drawn into union with souls of the Church Triumphant, or, what is the same thing, the living with the dead.

All that I have said is psychological reasoning, but if we open Holy Scripture we can verify the truth of it. (1) Jesus Christ says to the Apostle Peter, "I have prayed for thee, that thy faith fail not." There you see that the power of Christ's prayer strengthens the spirit of St. Peter and encourages him when his faith is tested. (2) When the Apostle Peter was kept in prison, "prayer was made without ceasing of the Church unto God for him." Here we have revealed the help which brotherly prayer gives in the troubled circumstances of life. (3) But the clearest precept about prayer for others is put by the Holy Apostle James in this way: "Confess your sins one to another, and pray for one another... The effectual fervent prayer of a righteous man availeth much." Here is definite confirmation of the psychological argument above. And what are we to say of the example of the Holy Apostle Paul, which is given to us as the pattern of prayer for one another? One writer observes that this example of the Holy Apostle Paul should teach us how necessary prayer for one another is, when so holy and strong a podvizhnik acknowledges his own need of this spiritual help. In the Epistle to the Hebrews he words his request in this way: "Pray for us: for we trust we have a good conscience, in all things willing to live honestly" (Heb. 13:18). When we take note of this, how unreasonable it seems to rely upon our own prayers and successes only, when a man so holy, so full of grace, in his humility asks for the prayers of his neighbors (the Hebrews) to be joined to his own. Therefore, in humility, simplicity, and unity of love we should not reject or disdain the help of the prayers of even the feeblest of believers, when the clear-sighted spirit of the Apostle Paul felt no hesitation about it. He asks for the prayers of all in general, knowing that the power of God is made perfect in weakness. Consequently it can at times be made perfect in those who seem able to pray but feebly. Feeling the force of this example, we notice further that prayer one for another strengthens that unity in Christian love which is commanded by God, witnesses to humility in the spirit of him who makes the request, and, so to speak, attracts the spirit of him who prays. Mutual intercession is stimulated in this way.

The Professor. Your analysis and your proofs are admirable and exact, but it would be interesting to hear from you the actual method and form of prayer for others. For I think that if the fruitfulness and attractive power of prayer depend upon a living interest in our neighbors, and conspicuously upon the constant influence of the spirit of him who prays upon the spirit of him who asked for prayer, such a state of soul might draw one away from the uninterrupted sense of the invisible presence of God and the outpouring of one's soul before God in one's own needs. And if one brings one's neighbor to mind just once or twice in the day, with sympathy for him, asking the help of God for him, would that not be enough for the attracting and strengthening of his soul? To put it briefly, I should like to know exactly how to pray for others.

The Monk. Prayer which is offered to God for anything whatever ought not, and cannot, take us away from the sense of the presence of God, for if it is an offering made to God, then, of course, it must be in His presence. So far as the method of praying for others is concerned, it must be noted that the power of this sort of prayer consists in true Christian sympathy with one's neighbor, and it has an influence upon his soul according to the extent of that sympathy. Therefore, when one happens to remember him (one's neighbor), or at the time appointed for doing so, it is well to bring a mental view of him into the presence of God, and to offer prayer in the following form: "most merciful God, Thy will be done, which will have all men to be saved and to come unto the knowledge of the truth, save and help Thy servant N. Take this desire of mine as a cry of love which Thou hast commanded." Commonly you will repeat those words when your soul feels moved to do so, or you might say this prayer using your Prayer Rope. I have found from experience how beneficially such a prayer acts upon him for whom it is offered.

The Professor. Your views and arguments and the edifying conversation and illuminating thoughts which spring from them are such that I shall feel bound to keep them in my memory, and to give you all the reverence and thanks of my grateful heart.

The Pilgrim Continues His Way

The Pilgrim and the Professor. The time has come for us to go. Most heartily we ask for your prayers upon our journey and upon our companionship.

The Starets. "The God of peace that brought again from the dead our Lord Jesus, that great Shepherd of the sheep, though the Blood of the Everlasting Convenant, make you perfect in every good work to do His will, working in you that which is well pleasing in His sight, through Jesus Christ; to whom be glory for ever and ever. Amen" (Heb. 13:20, 21) .

Directives on Prayer of the Heart

St. Simeon the New Theologian

Interior Prayer is truly marvelous but it is difficult to explain. For those without practical experience it seems not only incomprehensible but incredible. In fact, this form of prayer is very rare in our times because the snares of the devil entrap man in all forms of distraction, and pure prayer can only be offered to God when the mind is free of all distracting thoughts.

The following conditions are necessary for success in this form of prayer: perfect obedience; guarding the purity of one's conscience in regard to God, to neighbor, and to objects; and a resolve to walk in the presence of God. If you proceed in this manner, you will prepare for yourself a direct path for interior prayer.

Your mind should guard your heart in time of prayer; the mind should constantly descend into the heart and from the depths of the heart offer up prayer to God.

You should do all this until such time as you taste the sweetness of the Lord. When finally the mind is in the heart and it tastes how sweet the Lord is, then it will not wish to leave the heart but will say with St. Peter, "Lord, it is wonderful for us to be here" (Matt. 17:4); then the mind will constantly look into the heart, and if it wanders, it will return there again and again and will repel the thoughts brought by the devil.

For those who have no knowledge and understanding of this inner activity it will seem difficult and oppressive. But those who have tasted the sweetness of the Lord in prayer will cry with St. Paul, "Nothing

therefore can come between us and the love of Christ"
(Rom 8:35).

Therefore, our Holy Fathers, who heard from the
Lord that "from the heart come evil intentions: murder,
adultery, fornication, theft, perjury, slander. These are
the things that make a man unclean" (Matt. 15:19-20),
also heard in another part of the Gospel that we should
"clean the inside of the cup and dish first so that the
outside may become clean as well" (Matt. 23:26). The
Fathers abandoned every other spiritual pursuit and
began wholeheartedly to practice this one activity, the
guarding of the heart; for they were convinced that
through this holy occupation they would easily attain
every virtue, but without it they would not attain any.
This was their predominant occupation and they also
wrote about it. He who wishes should read the writings
of St. Mark the Hermit, John Climacus, Hesychius of
Jerusalem, Philotheus of Sinai, Abba Isaiah,
Barsanuphius the Great, and others.

If you wish to learn how to descend into the heart
and remain there I will tell you.

First you must observe the following three
conditions: You must be free from all cares, not only
vain and unholy cares but even good things. In other
words, you should be dead to everything; your
conscience should be pure and it should not denounce
you in anything. You should be completely free from
passionate attachments; your thoughts should not be
inclined toward anything worldly. Then sit alone in a
quiet place, close the door, take your mind from every
temporal and vain thing, bow your head toward your
chest and stay attentively inside of yourself, not in the
head but in the heart, and holding the mind there with

your inner eyes watch your breathing. With your mind find the place of the heart and let it abide there. In the beginning you will experience darkness and discomfort, but if you will continue this activity of attention without interruption, you will attain unceasing joy. If the mind continues with this activity, it will find the place of the heart and will see things it never knew and saw before. Then, no matter what distracting thoughts would come, it will immediately repel and destroy them through the Name of Jesus. From this time also the mind will experience anger toward the demons and will pursue and overcome them. In addition what usually follows from this you will learn by experience if with the help of God you will guard your attention and keep your mind on the prayer "Lord Jesus Christ, have mercy on me!"

St. Gregory of Sinai

Having received the spirit of Jesus Christ by means of a pure Prayer of the Heart, we should communicate mystically with the Lord. But not understanding the greatness, honor, and glory resulting from grace and not caring about our spiritual growth through the keeping of the commandments and reaching true contemplation, we are careless and therefore fall into sensual habits and we throw ourselves into the abyss of insensitivity and darkness. It happens also that we think very little of God's presence and do not realize that we should be as rays of grace. We believe but not with a living faith, and despite the new spirit which we receive in Baptism, we do not cease to live according to the flesh. If we do repent and begin to keep the commandments, we keep only the letter of the law and not the spirit and we are so alienated from spiritual life that even when we see it in others we imagine it as error and confusion. In this way we are dead in the spirit, alive but not in Christ and not in accordance with the conviction that what is born of the spirit should be spiritual.

However, what we have received in holy Baptism of the life of Jesus Christ is not destroyed but is only buried as some treasure in the earth. But wisdom and grace demand a concern about this in order to reveal it and bring it into the open. But how?

Two methods can lead us to this actualization: In the first place, this gift is open to the one who keeps the commandments; and to the degree that we keep the commandments, we experience light and wisdom. In the second place, the method by which we can acquire this gift is ceaseless calling on the Lord Jesus or constant awareness of God's presence. The first means is powerful, but the second is even more powerful and it supports the first. Therefore, if we sincerely wish to reveal the abundance of grace buried in us, we will hasten to acquire the habit of the second method, the Prayer of the Heart, and we will practice this imageless activity until it warms our heart and enflames it to unspeakable love for the Lord.

The action of this Prayer in the Heart can be present in two ways: sometimes the mind anticipates and attaches itself to the Lord in the heart by continual remembrance; at other times the Prayer comes first in sparks of joy, attracts the mind to the heart, and binds it to call on the Lord Jesus in reverential presence before Him. In the first case the action of the Prayer can be noticed in the subduing of the passions through keeping of the commandments and the warmth of the heart which results from diligent calling on the Lord Jesus; in the second case the spirit attracts the mind to the heart

Directives on Prayer of the Heart

and holds it there in the depths, keeping it from its usual wandering. From these two aspects of the prayer the mind is either active or contemplative; when active it overcomes the passions with the help of God, and when contemplative it sees God as it is possible for a man to do.

The active Prayer of the Heart and the mind can be accomplished in the following way: Sitting on a chair, bring your mind from the head into the heart and hold it there; from there call with your mind and heart, "Lord Jesus Christ, have mercy on me!" Regulate your breathing also, because rhythmic breathing can disperse distracting thoughts. When you are aware of thoughts, do not pay attention to them regardless of whether they are good or not. With your mind enter the heart and call on the Lord Jesus often and patiently and in this way you will soon overwhelm and destroy these thoughts through God's Name. St. John Climacus says that with the Name of Jesus you can destroy the enemy, for a more powerful weapon does not exist either in heaven or on earth.

When the mind becomes exhausted by such effort and the body and heart is weak from frequent calling on the Lord Jesus, you can stand and sing; or you can think about some passage from the Scripture or about death, or you can read, do manual work, or do some other thing.

When you take upon yourself this activity of prayer, then you should read only those books which contain teachings about interior life, about temperance and prayer, namely the works of St. John Climacus, Isaac of Syria, the ascetical books of Maximus the Confessor, Simeon the New Theologian, Hesychius, Philotheus of

Directives on Prayer of the Heart

Sinai, other similar writings. Leave the writings about other matters for a while, not because they are not good but because they are not appropriate to study when you aspire to keep your mind on prayer. Read only a little but deeply and try to assimilate what you read.

Do not abandon prayer books. Some people hold on to many methods of prayer found in prayer books while others give up prayer books completely and concentrate only on mental prayer. You should take the middle road: Do not say many prayers because you will be exhausted; but do not give them up altogether because of infirmity and weakness. If you see that the prayer is active in you and its movement does not cease in your heart, do not leave it and take a prayer book. This would be the same as if you left God in the depths of your heart and then tried to converse with him from the outside. For those who do not yet have self-activating prayer it is necessary to say many words, even without measure, in order to be in this prayerful atmosphere unceasingly until such an intense prayerful effort inflames the heart and begins self-activating prayer. He who finally tastes this sweetness should then shorten his active prayer and concentrate more on mental prayer as the Fathers suggest. When you become interiorly weak, it is necessary to pray actively or to read the writings of the Fathers. Oars are not necessary when the winds keep the boat in full sail; they are needed when the wind subsides and leaves the boat.

A spirit of contrition is a great weapon against the enemy so that one does not give in to conceit because of the consolations received in prayer. He who guards the spirit of contrition avoids all manner of difficulties. Real and not imagined interior prayer is that in which the warmth from the Prayer of Jesus comes, brings fire

Directives on Prayer of the Heart

to the sphere of the heart, and burns the passions like weeds. It consoles the soul with joy and peace and comes not from the left or from the right or from on high but proceeds from the heart as the source of living water of the life-giving Spirit. Aspire to keep this Spirit in your heart by always guarding the mind from images. When united to the Spirit do not be afraid of anything, because He who said, "Courage, it is I, do not be afraid," is Himself with you.

St. Nicephorus the Solitary

You wish to perceive the heavenly fire sensible in your heart and to know by experience that the Kingdom of Heaven is within you, come and I will tell you about the science of heavenly life, or better about the art which can lead him who practices it, without labor and sweat, into the refuge of passionlessness. Through our fall we entered into it; now let us return to ourselves by renouncing our passions. We cannot be reconciled with God and be intimate with Him if we will not first return to ourselves and enter into the depths of ourselves. Only tho interior life is a truly Christian life. All the Fathers give witness to this.

Once a brother asked Abba Agathon what is more important--physical work or guarding of the heart. The wise man replied that man is similar to a tree: the physical work can be compared to the leaves and guarding of the heart to the fruit. Therefore, according to Scripture, every tree which does not produce good fruit is to be cut down and thrown into the fire (Matt 3:10). So it is evident that you ought to turn your attention on the fruit, that is the guarding of the heart.

Directives on Prayer of the Heart

However, we need also the adornment of the leaves or physical work.

St. John Climacus says, "Close the door of your cell to your body, the door of your lips to conversation, and the inner door of your soul to evil spirits. Sitting on high--that is, having attained attention in the heart--observe, if you are tempted, what kind and how many robbers come in order to enter into the garden of your heart and steal grapes. When the guard gets tired, he gets up to pray, then again sits down and with renewed courage begins again the attention of the heart and prayer.

St. Macarius the Great teaches that the most important work of the ascetic is to enter one's heart and to war against Satan and guard against his evil thoughts.

St. Isaac of Syria writes, "Endeavor to enter into your inner treasure house and you will see a heavenly treasure. The ladder leading into the kingdom of heaven is hidden within you, in your heart. And so purify yourself from sin and enter your heart; there you will find the rungs of the ladder by which you can climb to the heights."

And St. John Carpathos says, "Much labor and effort is needed in prayer in order to acquire a peaceful state of the mind and thoughts, that other heaven of the heart where Christ lives. As the Apostle Paul says, 'Do you acknowledge that Jesus Christ is really in you?' (2 Cor. 13:5)."

St. Simeon the New Theologian has this to say: "From the time when man was banished from paradise and alienated himself from God, Satan and his angels

230

received freedom to tempt man night and day. There is no other way for the mind to free itself from this than by constant remembrance of God. He who walks in the presence of God is strengthened in mental silence and the guarding of the heart." All the Holy Fathers teach this. This, the greatest of all activities can be learned through study. Few receive this gift directly from God because of the fervor of their faith. Therefore it is necessary to look for a director who knows this activity. But if there is no such director, then call on God for help with a contrite and humble heart and do what I will tell you.

You know that breathing brings air into the heart. And so sit quietly and take your mind and lead it by the path of breathing into the very heart and hold it there; do not give it freedom to escape as it would wish to. While holding it there do not leave your mind idle but give it the following holy words to say: "Lord Jesus Christ, Son of God, have mercy on me!" And let the mind repeat them day and night. Try to get accustomed to this inner dwelling with the assigned prayer and do not allow your mind to leave the heart too soon, because at the beginning it will get very tired and lonely in such interior confinement. Then when it gets used to it, the mind will be happy and joyful to be there and it will want of itself to stay there. Just as a man who returns home from a foreign country is beside himself with joy at seeing his wife and children, in like manner the mind, when it is united with the heart, is full of unspeakable joy and delight.

When you are successful in entering the heart by this means which I have shown you, give thanks to God and continue with this activity unceasingly, for it will teach you what you cannot learn in any other way. If, however, after trying hard you do not succeed in entering the realm of the heart by this means which I have described, then do what I will now suggest and with God's help you will find what you seek. You know that man communicates with himself interiorly in the breast. When the lips are silent we converse with ourselves, we pray, recite psalms, and lead different forms of conversation with ourselves. You can control this inner talking and instruct your mind to banish every thought and say, "Lord Jesus Christ, Son of God, have mercy on me." Force yourself to repeat this cry constantly. Patiently continue with this activity for some time, and a way to the heart will be opened for you without any doubt. We have learned this by experience.

If you do this with great desire and attention, the entrance into the heart will bring about a host of virtues: love, joy, peace, long-suffering, humility, and others.

Sts. Callistus and Ignatius

Fervor and zeal to live according to Christ's commandments and to show forth that perfection which we received in Baptism are the beginning of spiritual life. "You must give up your old way of life; you must put aside your old self, which gets corrupted by following illusory desires. Your mind must be renewed by a spiritual revolution so that you can put on the new self that has been created in God's way, in the goodness and holiness of the truth" (Eph. 4:22-24). This holiness and truth in us is the Lord Jesus Christ; as St. Paul tells us, "I must go through the pain of giving birth to you all over again, until Christ is formed in you" (Gal. 4:19).

St. John Chrysostom says that when we were baptized, our soul became brighter than the sun, for we

232

Directives on Prayer of the Heart

were purified by the Holy Spirit. As polished silver illumined by the rays of the sun radiates light, so the soul purified in Baptism receives the rays of glory from the Spirit and reflects this glory. But alas! this unspeakable and awesome glory is in us only one or two days and then we extinguish it by flooding it in a storm of earthly cares and passions.

In the divine womb, that is in the holy font, we received God's Holy Grace. And if we cover it in the darkness of earthly cares and passions, then we can get it back by repentance, by keeping God's commandments and can again see its supernatural brightness. This grace is manifested to the measure of each man's zeal and living faith, but especially through the intercession of our Lord Jesus Christ. St. Mark says that Christ gave to the baptized the Grace of the Holy Spirit, which needs no supplement from us; it simply reveals itself in us and becomes visible according to the measure of our keeping of the commandments and until we reach the fullness of Christ.

As has been said, the principle and the root of all spiritual activity is to live according to the commandments of the Lord, and the end and fruit of this is to recapture the grace of the Holy Spirit which was given to us in Baptism but which is buried under passions. Therefore it behooves us to try with zeal to keep the commandments so that God's grace can again shine brightly in us. John, the Beloved Disciple of the Lord, says, "Whoever keeps His commandments lives in God and God lives in him" (1 John 3:24). And the Lord Himself teaches, "If anyone loves Me he will keep My word, and My Father will love him, and We shall come to him and make Our home with him" (John 14:23).

Without the help of Jesus Christ it is impossible for us to fulfill the commandments perfectly, for He Himself says, "Without Me you can do nothing" (John 15:5). And St. Peter said, "Of all the names in the world given to men this is the only one by which we can be saved" (Acts 4:12). He is for us the Way, the Truth, and the Life. Therefore, filled with the Holy Spirit, our glorious teachers and guides wisely tell us to give prayer to Jesus the first place in our lives, with great trust to ask Him for grace by calling on His Name constantly, and to stay united with Him whether we eat or drink, sleep or are awake. Because away from Him things will go wrong for us, but united to Him all good will come to us. "Whoever remains in Me, with Me in him, bears fruit in plenty" (John 15:5).

And so, aware of our weakness and placing all our trust in the Lord, we should love His commandments more than life and direct all our attention to acquiring the habit of ceaseless calling on the Name of the Lord. This activity will dispel all evil and bring all good. In order to accomplish this the Holy Fathers recommend one special activity, which they call an art and even the art of arts. We present here the natural method of St. Nicephorus of entering the heart by means of breathing which contributes toward the concentration of thoughts. These are his instructions: "Sitting down in a quiet place take your mind and lead it into the heart by the path of breathing and, keeping it there attentively, say without ceasing, 'Lord Jesus Christ, have mercy on me!' Do this until the activity in the heart becomes natural and ceaseless."

Directives on Prayer of the Heart

This is what all the Fathers taught. St. John Chrysostom says, "I entreat you, brother, never to stop reciting this prayer." And in another place he says that everyone should say the Prayer no matter what he is doing; whether he eats, drinks, sits, serves, or travels, he should not cease reciting the Prayer, and the Name of the Lord Jesus Christ will descend into the depths of the heart, will subdue the pernicious serpent, and will regenerate and save the soul. Abide in unceasing calling of the Name Lord Jesus so that the heart can absorb the Lord and the Lord the heart and the two become one. And, also, do not separate your heart from God but always guard in it the memory of our Lord Jesus Christ, until the Name of the Lord is rooted in the depths of the heart and you do not think of anything else, so that Christ will be exalted in you. St. John Climacus says, "May the memory of Jesus be united with your breathing." And St. Hesychius writes, "If you wish to cover with confusion distracting thoughts and to guard your heart, let the Jesus Prayer be attuned to your breathing, and in a few days you will see your desire accomplished."

If we train the mind to descend into the heart with the breath, we will note that the mind will concentrate only on calling on our Lord Jesus Christ. However, when it leaves the heart and gives itself to external occupations, the mind will become divided and distracted. Therefore, to safeguard the singleness of purpose, the experienced Fathers suggest that the beginner should sit in a quiet and dimly lit room for this exercise, since seeing external objects is distracting, whereas in a quiet and dimly lit place the mind becomes still and collected within itself. As St. Basil says, "A mind which is not distracted and dispersed through the senses returns to itself."

Note carefully, however, that the essence of this achievement consist in an earnest and undistracted calling on our Lord Jesus Christ and not merely on the descent into the heart by way of breathing and sitting in a seclude and dimly lit place. The Holy Fathers set forth these and similar suggestions as aides to recollection. From the habit of being recollected and attentive is born the habit of pure prayer of the mind and heart.

All these suitable conditions are described in detail and are considered necessary until pure and continuous prayer is achieved in the heart. When in God's good time and with the grace of our Lord Jesus Christ you attain this form of prayer and are united with the Lord, then you can disregard all those helpful conditions.

And so, if in reality you wish to be made worthy of the life of Jesus Christ, strive to attain this that at all times and in every place and every activity you pray purely and earnestly to the Lord in your heart so that by this means you may grow into spiritual manhood, "until we become the perfect Man, fully mature with the fullness of Christ himself" (Eph. 4:13). And do not forget, when pure prayer is active in you, that you do not under any circumstance allow your rules on prayer to interfere with this. If day or night the Lord makes you worthy of experiencing pure and undistracted prayer, then disregard your rules and with all your strength attach yourself to the Lord God, and He will enlighten your heart in your spiritual activity.

When you will be worthy of the gift of ceaseless prayer in the heart, then, according to St. Isaac of Syria, you will have reached the summit of all virtues and become a dwelling place of the Holy Spirit; then the prayer will not cease, whether you sit, walk, eat, drink, or do anything else. Even in deep sleep prayer will be active in you without any effort, for even when it is externally silent, it continues secretly to act within.

St. Hesychius of Jerusalem

Recollection is freedom from all thoughts and continuous silence of the heart. It constantly breathes in Christ Jesus, Son of God, and Him alone. With Him it bravely fights against enemies and confesses to Him who has the power to forgive sins.

Recollection is a firm control of the mind which is posted at the door of the heart so that it sees the robbers, the alien thoughts, as they come, and hears what these enemies say and do; how the demons present images as they try to seduce the mind by fantasy. If this work is done with loving effort, it will teach us the art of mental war.

The first method of recollection is to watch the imagination or suggestion closely. The second is always to keep the heart deeply silent, to still all thoughts and pray. The third is to call humbly and ceaselessly on our Lord Jesus Christ for help. The fourth is to keep death constantly before one's eyes. And the fifth and best is to look only to heaven, disregarding everything earthly.

He who struggles inwardly must constantly practice these four acts: humility, strict recollection, resistance to thoughts, and prayer. Humility because, since the struggle is against proud demons, man is in constant need of help from Christ, who hates the proud.

Directives on Prayer of the Heart

Recollection in order to keep the heart free from all thoughts, even the seemingly good. Resistance so that, when he distinguishes clearly who it is that comes to him, he may at once with firmness repel the evil one; as it is said: "I can find an answer to the insults, since I rely on your word" (Ps. 119:42). Prayer so that after resistance he may immediately cry from the depths of his heart to Christ with unutterable groaning. Then he that struggles will see how the enemy is confused in his images by the Holy Name of Jesus, just as dust is scattered by the wind or smoke is blown away.

He who has no prayer that is free from distractions has no weapon for battle; this is the prayer which is continuously active in the innermost places of the soul, the calling on the Name of our Lord Jesus Christ, who flogs and scorches the invisible enemy.

With a keen and intense gaze of the mind you should look within in order to see those who enter; and when you see them, you should at once crush the head of the snake by resistance, and if you call on Christ, you will experience divine intercession.

If in the spirit of humility and remembrance of death you reproach yourself, resist distracting thoughts, and remain in your heart constantly calling on Jesus Christ and if you persevere on this narrow but sweet path of the mind, you will reach a state of contemplation, and will be enlighten about the deep mysteries of Christ, "until you really know God's secret in which all the jewels of wisdom and knowledge are hidden" (Col. 2:3). For through Jesus you will also receive the Holy Spirit, who will enable you to see the glory of the Lord with an unveiled face (2 Cor. 3:18).

Directives on Prayer of the Heart

"Your enemy the devil is prowling round like a roaring lion, looking for someone to devour" (1 Pet. 5:8). Therefore, be vigilant and attentive, resist distracting thoughts, and be faithful in your prayer to Christ Jesus, our God. For no one can help you more than Jesus our Lord and God, who knows all the cunning tricks and snares of the devil.

As salt enhances the taste of bread and all food, and even preserves meat from decaying, so you should resolve to guard the inner savor of the mind and the wonderful activity in the heart, for it will bring divine sweetness to both the inner and the outer man, drive away wicked thoughts, and preserve you continually in what is good.

The fervor of your prayer will be determined by the recollection of your mind. And to the degree that you are careless in recollecting your mind, to that same degree you will be alienated from Jesus. And as perfect recollection brightly illumines the mind, so lack of it and of fervent calling on Jesus makes it completely dark.

Unceasing and fervent calling on Jesus, full of sweetness and joy, brings a delightful stillness to the heart. But it is only Jesus Christ, the Son of God and author of all good, who can purify the heart perfectly, for He says, "I it was who roused him to victory, I leveled the way for him" (Is. 45:13).

A heavenly state will be born in our mind if we do not neglect ceaseless prayer and continual recollection as a necessary condition, but remember to call on our Lord Jesus Christ. And indeed this is how we should always be calling upon Jesus Christ our Lord; with a burning heart we should cry to Him to be made worthy to taste the sweetness of His Name. For frequent practice is the mother of a habit both in virtue and in vice, and a habit becomes second nature. When the mind attains such a state, it seeks its enemies of its own accord, as a hound seeks a hare in a thicket. But whereas the hound seeks it preys to devour it, the mind tries to strike it down and drive it away.

David, who was both wise and experienced in deeds, said to the Lord, "My Strength, I look to you" (Ps. 59:9). Thus it is that the Lord's strength preserves in us that silence of heart and mind from which all virtues proceed. The Lord gives us the commandments, and if we constantly call on Him, He protects us from negligence and forgetfulness, which are as destructive to our peace of heart as water is of fire. Therefore, do not allow negligence to overtake you but destroy your enemies with the Name of Jesus. Let His sweet Name be joined to your breath and then you will know the value of silence.

The most wonderful fruit of mental silence is that sinful thoughts that knock at the door of the mind, which would, if admitted, become evil deeds, are cut off by the mind and the intercession of our Lord Jesus Christ.

Once we have begun to live attentively in humility and recollection and prayer, we will make progress on out mental journey with the holy Name of Jesus Christ, which will light our way like a lamp. However, if we place our trust in ourselves and our ability to be recollected, we will be quickly attacked and overcome by the enemy. Then the enemy will begin to overpower us in everything and we will find ourselves enmeshed in evil desires as in a net, or we shall be completely destroyed by the enemy since we will not have with us the victorious Name of Jesus Christ. For it is only this sacred weapon, when it is constantly wielded in a heart which is free from all images, that can turn them to flight, slay and scorch them, and devour them as fire devours straw.

St. Philotheus of Sinai

The goal of one who strives after righteousness, on which his mind should be firmly set, is to treasure the presence of God in his heart as a priceless pearl or some other precious jewel. He should disregard everything, even his present life, for the sake of having God in his heart.

From early morning it is necessary to guard the door of one's heart courageously and steadfastly with keen awareness of God's presence and ceaseless pray to Jesus Christ in the soul. By this mental vigilance we should cut off the heads of our enemy and destroyed the very first sign of disturbing thoughts and allow God's presence to raise us on high.

Recollection is rightly called a way, as it leads us into the kingdom within as well as to the future one. It is also called the workshop of the mind, for it perfects and transforms our mental character and destroys our passions. Recollection is also similar to a window through which God enters and manifests Himself to the mind.

Where there is humility, awareness of God's presence, recollection, and frequent prayer directed

241

against the enemy, there is God's abode where hosts of demons fear to enter.

The first door leading into the Jerusalem of the mind or mental silence is the external silence of the lips; the second is abstinence from food, drink, and sleep; and the third door which purifies both the body and the mind, is meditation on death.

Awareness of God's presence, that is of Jesus, together with heartfelt contrition, can annihilate all the fascinating thoughts, the variety of suggestions, dreams, gloomy imaginings, and everything with which the all-destructive enemy arms himself and comes forth daringly seeking to devour our souls. When Jesus is invoked, He easily destroys all these, for there is no salvation except in Jesus Christ. The Savior Himself confirmed this when He said, "Without Me you can do nothing" (John 15:5).

And so every hour and every moment let us guard our heart from thoughts that obscure the mirror of our soul, which should only reflect the radiant image of Jesus Christ, who is the Wisdom and the Power of God the Father. Let us continuously seek the kingdom within our heart and we will certainly find the seed, the pearl, and the yeast and everything else if we purify the eye of our mind; for Christ said, "The Kingdom of God is within you" (Luke 17:21).

St. Theoleptus, Metropolitan of Philadelphia

When the sun sets night comes, and when Christ leaves the soul the darkness of passions envelops it and mental beasts come to devour it. When the sun rises beasts hide in their holes, and when Christ rises in the

Directives on Prayer of the Heart

praying heart all desire for worldly pleasure ceases, pity for the flesh vanishes, and the mind goes forth to do its work to think of God till evening.

Put an end to conversations with the outer world until you find the place of pure prayer and the home in which Christ dwells, who enlightens and gladdens you by His knowledge and visitation.

Footsteps on the snow vanish, for they either are melted by rays of the sun or are washed away by rains; and memories of deeds and objects of sensual pleasures are annihilated either by Christ, who shines forth in the heart through prayer, or when the rain of tears of sincere contrition comes.

Remain in the privacy of your holy dwelling place and strive from there to enter the innermost watchtower of the soul, where Christ abides, bringing you peace, joy, and untroubled stillness. These are the gifts of Christ, the inner Sun which He sends forth like rays and bestows as a reward upon a soul which welcomes Him.

In your progress of mental prayer call on the Lord constantly and never lose heart. Pray steadfastly like the importunate widow who moved the implacable judge to mercy. Then it will be obvious that you walk in the spirit and do not pay attention to the lusts of the flesh and do not interrupt the ceaseless flow of prayer by worldly thoughts but live as a temple of God in which He is praised without distraction. If you continue to practice mental prayer, then you will attain constant awareness of God's presence and the inaccessible hidden treasure of the mind. In contemplation you will see Him who is unseen; you will serve the one God and in solitude you will pour out your heart to Him.

Sts. Barsanuphius and John

When you call on God's Name, you weaken your enemies. Knowing this, do not cease to call on God's Name for help. This is what prayer is, and Scripture says that we should pray constantly (1 Thess. 5:17).

Remember that God knows the hearts of men and looks into them, so call on Him in your heart. This is what is meant in Scripture; "But when you pray, go to your private room and, when you have shut your door, pray to your Father who is in that secret place" (Matt. 6:6). Let us close our lips and pray to Him in out heart, because he who closes his lips and calls on God, or prays to Him in his heart, is the one who fulfills the commandment of the Lord.

The effort of your heart should consist in this, to pray unceasingly to God. If you wish to succeed in this, then begin to strive earnestly and in hope, and God will bless you with success.

Ceaseless calling on God's Name is a medicine which destroys not only the passions but also their activity. As a doctor finds the right medicine or bandage for a wound and these help though the sick man does not know how, the same is true with God, for when He is called upon, He annihilates all passions though we do not know how.

The Lord said, "Ask, and it will be given to you" (Luke 11:9). Pray to the All-Good God that He sends you the Holy Spirit, the Comforter, and He will teach you everything and reveal all mysteries to you. Take Him as your leader and He will not allow deception to enter your heart; he will dispel distraction, negligence, and drowsiness in your mind. He will enlighten your eyes, strength your heart, and raise your mind. Cling to Him, believe in Him, and love Him.

Abba Philemon

By means of silence you can thoroughly cleanse your mind and give it constant spiritual occupation. As the eye turned on sensory objects looks closely at what it sees, so a pure mind turned toward spiritual things is uplifted by the object of its contemplation. The mind becomes perfect when it enters into the sphere of essential knowledge and is united with God. Having thus attained kingly rank, the mind is no longer poor and it is not carried away by false desires, even if all the kingdoms of the world were offered to it.

Above all strive to guard your mind and practice recollection; be patient in difficult circumstances and try at all costs to preserve the spiritual blessings which you have acquired. Be attentive and diligent and do not give in to lusts which secretly try to steal in. For although silence tames the passions of the soul, if they are allowed to flare up and become acute they can lead you into sin.

Even when satisfying your most urgent needs, do not allow your mind to be idle but compel it to continue secretly to learn and to pray. In this way you will be able to understand the depth of the Divine Scripture and the power which is concealed in it.

Brief Directives for Prayer of the Heart

1. Sit or stand in a dimly lit and quiet place.

2. Recollect yourself.

3. With the help of your imagination find the place of the heart and stay there with attention.

4. Lead the mind from the head into the heart and say, "Lord Jesus Christ, have mercy on me," quietly with the lips or mentally, whichever is more convenient; say the prayer slowly and reverently.

5. As much as possible guard the attention of your mind and do not allow any thoughts to enter it.

6. Be patient and peaceful.

7. Be moderate in food, drink, and sleep.

8. Learn to love silence.

9. Read the Scriptures and the writings of the Fathers about prayer.

10. As much as possible avoid distracting occupations.

Our Fathers in Christ

Schema-monk Theodore
b. Mar 19, 1905 † November 20, 1996

Bishop Constantine (Jesensky)
b. May 30, 1907 † May 31, 1996

Notes:

Notes:

Notes: